SKYSCRAPER

TO THOSE FIGHTING FOR LIFE

This book is dedicated to the Palestinian health workers in Gaza. To all the ambulance crews, nurses, doctors, medical students and volunteers who fought to protect the lives of those who fought to save the lives of those who were wounded or unhurt, the living and the dying, often putting their own lives on the line, throughout the fifty-one days of the major Israeli offensive in the summer of 2014.

DO NOT LOSE YOUR WAY

'With our choice of profession, we have chosen to take the side of life. This means individual initiative, creative enthusiasm, courage and spontaneity.

Others take the side of death. That implies acting with systematic, calculated deviousness, as well as the repudiation of youth. As doctors, we only have one loyalty, and that is towards the individual patient whom fate has brought to us. If you manage to stick to that thought, you cannot lose your way, not even in the clouded moral landscape of modern life.'

Prof. Anton Hauge
From his speech to graduating medical students at the University of Oslo, 1995

CONTENTS

PREFACE:
TESTIMONY

THIS BOOK IS A TESTIMONY, not an academic thesis or a neutral journalistic report.

This book is my account of what I witnessed in Gaza in the summer of 2014. It is the story of some of the human cost paid by the Palestinian people for enduring the Israeli occupation. For almost seventy years, they have been living under an increasingly brutal apartheid regime and constant military attacks. Many older Palestinians still remember what happened in 1948 in the *Nakba*, the Palestinian catastrophe, when the state of Israel was created on their land. Large parts of the population in what was once Palestine were driven from their homes, towns and villages by armed force and terror. Most of the Palestinians in Gaza are refugees in their own country.

The elderly generation who remember the *Nakba* say that the attack this summer was worse than 1948.

I have been carrying out medical solidarity work for the Palestinians since 1981. It has become a part of my life and a great source of joy and sorrow, inspiration and disappointment. For the past fifteen years, I have been working in Gaza with the Palestinian health service, making at least one trip a year to teach, organise projects, perform research, learn or carry out actual emergency medical treatment, especially in periods of war. Since 2006, I have witnessed at close hand four attacks by the Israeli military on the population of Gaza. Each time it happens,

I feel the anxiety coming over me at home in Norway. I know that I must go. Not because the Palestinians cannot manage their medical treatment by themselves – they are highly educated and have extensive experience dealing with medical care in war situations – but because of the importance of solidarity. 'It inspires us and strengthens us in our work,' they say. 'We're not alone when you come.'

The medical profession cannot and should not be detached from society; it should be a living force, a tool for living good lives and for making changes that serve justice. Medicine should be a peaceful weapon against oppression and injustice. Of course we have to take sides. We take the patients' side against whatever is detrimental to their health. This calls for action, often with political implications.

Life is sacred. Every single human life is irreplaceable, whosoever it is: Israeli or Palestinian, Norwegian or Afghan. For the Palestinians, whether they are in Gaza or the West Bank, in Israel or the diaspora, the circumstances of oppression they experience as a people under occupation are, in themselves, detrimental to their health. At the extreme, this might mean starvation caused by the siege, as well as death and trauma caused by the attacks.

I went to Gaza this summer to work at al-Shifa Hospital and show real solidarity. I am fortunate to have a job that can be useful in times of war. Modern weapons are horribly devious, causing terrific damage to the human body. When words alone are not enough, I take pictures, without disturbing our work, in order to be able to tell the people's story. If I am only securing airways, stopping bleeding, soothing pain and repairing wounds, I feel I am not doing enough. I have to do something about the fundamental injustices and distress experienced by the Palestinians. I want to tell people about the lives of those who are being bombed, life as it is experienced by the Palestinians themselves. I want to show the world the dignity, pride and indomitable, steadfast courage, the *sumūd* that these severely tested people have taught me about.

This book is one way of passing on my experiences of life in Gaza for fifteen days in July 2014. It is the photo story you will not see on television or in the newspapers. With a small, black camera ready in the pocket of my green operating scrubs, and with permission from the hospital management, I was able to take photographs freely, but naturally within accepted ethical limits.

What I experienced was awful, and it was immense. The sounds of bombs and screaming, bodies torn to pieces and a society reduced to rubble; but I also saw camaraderie, dignity, human courage and unflinching resolve.

I had no choice. I *had* to write.

The story of the Palestinians is best told by the Palestinians themselves. They rarely appear in the mainstream Western news sources, especially not in the United States, where the well-oiled and loudly voiced official Israeli account dominates, leaving no space for telling about the Palestinians' suffering or for self-critical analysis, just the usual claims about 'Palestinian terrorism' and Israeli 'self-defence'.

In each of the four Israeli assaults on Gaza over the past eight years, thousands of Palestinian civilians have been maimed or killed, and Palestinian society has been broken ever further apart. During the period from 2007 to today, Gaza has been subjected to a continuous Israeli siege and blockade, all with the full support of the United States, and to barely audible murmurs of opposition from Norway. After the most recent ceasefire in August 2014, Gaza is still behind the same suffocating blockade, on land as in the air and along the coast. No other regimes than the state of Israel would be able to get away with such an outrage without massive international criticism, political sanctions or threats of physical intervention. But Israel is wrapped up in an impenetrable protective blanket. Its political Teflon coating is carefully guarded by the Israeli government and significantly bolstered by the apparently unconditional support of the United States.

There is no major disagreement about the Israeli breaches of international law. According to a great number of global experts in international law, Israel is guilty of collective punishment, of the disproportionate use of force and of bombing civilian targets. Human rights organisations in Israel and Palestine – and elsewhere in the world – have thoroughly documented the injustices against the Palestinians and breaches of human rights, as have the United Nations. Resolutions have been adopted and verbal criticisms have been made by many governments, and yet the oppression of the Palestinian people continues in Gaza, in the West Bank and the diaspora. I have documented my own experiences from my work as a doctor in Gaza during the Israeli attacks in 2006, 2008–09, 2012 and most recently in 2014 in medical journals and books.

In Gaza, it is not primarily the military adversaries of the occupiers who are being killed and wounded. The overwhelming majority of casualties are civilian: men and women, children and young people, journalists, teachers, paramedics, fishermen, farmers and local politicians, to name but a few. Civil society lies in ruins after the fifty-one days of bombing. When the UN Secretary-General Ban Ki-moon visited Gaza on 14 October, on his way from the international donors' summit in Cairo, he said at a press conference that the destruction in Gaza was a 'source of pain' to him personally, and 'a shame to the international community'.

I do not support Hamas or Fatah. I support no Palestinian political parties or factions. I support the Palestinian people and their crystal clear right to oppose and resist a brutal occupier and an apartheid regime that is oppressing them in every area of their lives. I do not support attacks on civilian targets by anybody.

I am not neutral. I have taken a side. This book is a plea: in favour of the Palestinians, in favour of a fair political solution to the occupation of Palestine and in favour of a peaceful world.

As Archbishop Desmond Tutu has said: 'If you are neutral in situations of injustice, you have chosen the side of the oppressor.'

While I was working on this book, I set out on another journey back to Gaza.

This time, even though I had an Israeli visa valid for travel to Gaza, I was denied access through the Erez checkpoint by the Israeli authorities. This travel ban was later confirmed to the Norwegian Embassy in Tel Aviv, based on 'security grounds from the security authorities', and the ban is to have permanent effect. When a pen, a camera and a stethoscope are seen as security threats, we know we are dealing with a regime that is afraid of the truth and that believes power confers rights.

Mads Gilbert
Tromsø, 21 October 2014

THE HOME OF THE BRAVE

A Foreword by Max Blumenthal

WHEN A FIVE-DAY CEASEFIRE BETWEEN ISRAEL and Hamas took hold on 15 August, residents of Shuja'iyya were finally able to return to what was left of their homes. They pitched tents and erected signs asserting their claim to their property, sorting determinedly through the ruins of their lives.

Those who managed to survive the Israeli bombardment have come home to bedrooms obliterated by tank shells, kitchens pierced by Hellfire missiles, and boudoirs looted by soldiers who used their homes as bases of operations before embarking on a series of massacres. Once a solidly middle-class suburb of Gaza City comprised of multi-family apartments and stately homes, the neighborhood of Shuja'iyya had been transformed into a gigantic crime scene. It stood in the center of the long swath of Gaza Strip towns and cities that had been rendered uninhabitable by Israeli bombardment. All of these areas had one thing in common: they abutted the vast buffer zone the Israeli military had established between its border and the Gaza Strip. By pounding neighborhoods like Shuja'iyya and cities like Beit Hanoun until nearly all of their residents were forced to flee west for shelter, Israel was tightening the cage on the entire population.

The attack on Shuja'iyya began at 11.00 p.m. on 19 July, with a combined Israeli bombardment from F-16s, tanks and mortar launchers. As many as 140 fell under the bombardment, hundreds were injured, and none escaped unscathed by the indiscriminate violence. Inside the ruins of what used to be homes, returning locals related stories of survival and selflessness, detailing a harrowing night of death and destruction.

Outside a barely intact four-level, multi-family home that was hardly distinguishable from the other mangled structures lining the dusty roads of Shuja'iyya, I met members of the Atash family reclining on mats beside a makeshift stove. Khalil Atash, the sixty-three-year-old patriarch of the family, motioned to his son heating a teapot above a few logs and muttered: 'They've set us back a hundred years. Look at us, we're now burning wood to survive.'

Unlike most of their neighbors, who spent their nights sleeping in a squalid UN-run school, the Atashes had resolved to live in the only intact room of their home, a small bedroom on the top floor that was to have housed thirty-year-old Tamer and his wife. Just outside the room, the ceiling had been punctured by a 500 pound missile fired from an F-16. By a stroke of insane luck, the missile did not explode, sparing the family. The day before I arrived, a bomb disposal crew had defused its explosive charge.

Inside his bedroom, Tamer Atash described to me the night from hell, and how, despite everything, he and his family managed to survive.

'The missiles started getting closer and began to hit everywhere so randomly,' he recalled, detailing how the strikes on Shuja'iyya gradually intensified after the first hour. 'So I just lost it. I was watching my neighbors die and I was so close to them, I felt like I was dead too. I had two choices: either I die doing nothing at that house or do something about it. So I chose to do something.'

Tamer called an ambulance crew and begged the driver to help transport his family out of the attack. 'All I can do is pray for you,' the driver told him. But other first responders rushed headlong into the maelstrom, risking their lives to save as many of the fleeing residents as they could. By this time, the neighborhood was engulfed in flames and shrouded in darkness – Israeli forces had bombed all of its electricity towers. He and his family decided to burst into the street and make a blind dash. Neighbors followed closely behind them, embarking on a desperate sprint for survival as homes went up in flames around them.

Relying on cellphone flashlights to illuminate their path, the fleeing residents rushed ahead under withering shelling. Tens of people fell every few hundred meters,

Tamer told me. But they continued anyway, sprinting for a full kilometer until they reached safety close to Gaza City.

As soon as he reached sanctuary, Tamer said he was overcome with guilt. Friends and neighbors were stuck in the neighborhood with no one to evacuate them. He decided to return to help anyone he could. 'I'm from Shuja'iyya, I have no other place to go, and we don't own land,' he explained. 'This is our only place here. So of course I came back.'

It was well past midnight, Shuja'iyya was in flames, and the Qassam Brigades – the armed wing of Hamas – were beginning to mobilize for a counterattack. 'The situation outside was literally hell,' Tamer said.

In previous assaults on Gaza, Israeli forces met only light resistance. During Operation Cast Lead in 2008–09, when the army attacked Gaza's civilian population with indiscriminate firepower, most Israeli casualties were the result of so-called 'friendly fire.' But this time was different. With little more than light weapons at their disposal, uniformed Qassam fighters engaged the Israelis at close distances, sometimes just a few meters away, exposing a glaring weakness of the Middle East's most heavily equipped, technologically advanced armies. During the battle, Qassam fighters scored a hit on an Israeli armored personnel carrier, killing five soldiers inside, then captured the fatally wounded Staff Sergeant Oron Shaul.

The loss of soldiers and the possible capture of Shaul – a situation that raised the specter of a politically devastating prisoner swap – sent Israeli forces into a vengeful frenzy. 'The F-16s were no longer up in the sky bombing us, they were flying just above the houses,' Tamer recalled. 'It felt like an atomic bomb with four F-16s coming one way and another four from the opposite direction, weaving between the houses. At this point, we realized we were not surviving. We said our last prayers, and that was it. Because we know that when the Israelis lose one of their soldiers they become lunatics. We just knew they had suffered something, we could sense it.'

Tamer watched some of his neighbors jump from fourth-floor windows as their homes burst into flames. Others rushed out in their night clothes, nearly nude, prompting him and other men to hand over their shirts and even their trousers to women scurrying half exposed through the darkened streets. After giving the shirt off his back to one woman, he gave his sandals to another who had sliced her feet open on rubble.

'Sure, I was crazy and stupid, but I just wanted for them to survive,' he said. 'If I had to die, then fine, but someone had to make a sacrifice.'

By dawn, waves of survivors poured from Shuja'iyya into Gaza City. Sons had carried their fathers on their backs; mothers had hoisted children into lorries and ambulances; others searched frantically for missing family when they arrived, only to learn that they had fallen under the shelling. For many, it was another *Nakba*, a hellish reincarnation of the fateful days of 1948 when Zionist militias forcibly expelled hundreds of thousands of Palestinians from their land. This time, however, there was almost nowhere for the refugees to flee.

By dawn, a parade of ambulances was lined up at the gates of Gaza City's al-Shifa Hospital, unloading the wounded whose limbs had been chewed up by the hailstorm of Israeli shrapnel. In the distance, the deep thud of exploding shells could still be heard. Inside the hospital a corps of doctors and surgeons loomed over operating tables, their smocks spattered with the blood of small children. They worked under trying conditions, stretched to their limits by the deluge of casualties and deprived of adequate supplies by Israel's seven-year siege.

Among those who toiled inside al-Shifa was Mads Gilbert, a Norwegian doctor called to Gaza by his sense of duty. Gilbert had come from his home north of the Arctic Circle to treat those who had been left bare and vulnerable before the malevolent wrath of one of the world's most ruthless armies; to lend a hand to his colleagues in Gaza who, like the patients they treated, were stateless, dispossessed and denied rights by the top client of the world's lone superpower. As leaders from Washington to Westminster stood aside and watched the slaughter with cynical passivity, Gilbert sounded the alarm, alerting the world to the crisis unfolding before his eyes.

The pages of this book are comprised of Gilbert's recollections from inside the walls of al-Shifa during Gaza's darkest days, a time of emergency that summoned some of history's most astounding examples of human resilience and courage.

Max Blumenthal (b. 1977) is a prize-winning journalist and author living in the United States. His most recent book, Goliath: Life and Loathing in Greater Israel *(2013), takes a critical view of Israeli actions and has generated considerable debate.*

10. JULY

MIDNIGHT SUN
IN TROMSØ

THE MILD FÖHN WIND RUSHED THROUGH my hair, but otherwise everything was still. I was on ambulance helicopter duty out of Tromsø. The previous week I had come back from seventeen days spent in Gaza on behalf of the United Nations Relief and Works Agency for Palestine Refugees in the Near East (UNWRA) and the University Hospital of North Norway. Now Gaza had been replaced with the sea, the mountains, sky and sunshine. It was almost ten o' clock in the evening, and we had landed on a mountaintop with a majestic view. The thermometer showed it was 23°C. Summer in the Arctic!

'How about some supper up in the mountains while the weather's nice? We can train first and then eat afterwards.'

The whole crew was in agreement. I have been working with Roger and Tor Helge, the pilot and paramedic HEMS crew member respectively, for as long as I can remember. We make a good team and have been through a lot together. The on-call shifts last a week at a time and can involve anything from heart attacks to car accidents, births and burn injuries: the entire catalogue of emergency medicine, apart from war.

The Israeli assault on Gaza was now into its third day.

'I'm going back to Gaza tomorrow. They've asked me to go. The Managing Director Tor Ingebrigtsen has put me at their disposal,' I told the others.

'Do it for all of us,' they answered. 'Give our best wishes to our colleagues in Gaza, and come back safely.'

Everybody was willing to help out so I could go, even though there were still three days left of my shift.

'We support you,' is always the response from everybody at the University Hospital of North Norway, in Tromsø, my workplace of many years and a hospital genuinely committed to solidarity.

Passing through the sealed corridor from the Erez checkpoint in Israel to Gaza, under siege in occupied Palestine. The place is empty and deserted. I can hear the bombs and see black smoke rising into the sky. I walked past a TV cameraman, but otherwise nobody else is heading in.

13. JULY

INTO THE NIGHT

'WAIT OVER THERE, DON'T STOP HERE. Move!'

The young Israeli soldier behind the guardhouse's bullet-proof glass windows gestures impatiently towards the queue of people wanting a pass to Gaza. At the same time, explosions can be heard, and we see black smoke rising into the sky behind the concrete walls that separate Gaza from the rest of the world. It brings back bad memories.

The border crossing at Erez is chaotic. Several buses have driven right up to the barriers blocking the rest of the way to the border post itself, where the Israeli control systems are meticulously organised. Journalists are trying to get in, while representatives of foreign embassies and aid organisations are trying to get people out. There is an exodus of foreigners from Gaza, but most of those who live on this small strip of land cannot get out. The 1.7 million confined Palestinians have to stay, even though many would surely prefer to escape the increasingly intensive Israeli bombardment.

I am feeling tense. Will the Israelis let me in? It did not go according to plan yesterday when I tried to get into Gaza from Cairo, travelling through the Sinai Desert to the border crossing between Egypt and the southern end of Gaza at Rafah.

When I landed at the airport in Cairo yesterday morning, I met Dr. Mohammad Abou-Arab, a Norwegian-Palestinian anaesthetist who works at Aker University Hospital, in Oslo. He was with three other doctors from PalMed, an organisation of Palestinian doctors who work in Europe. Since we were all heading to Gaza, we took a taxi together. But we had barely got half-way before Egyptian soldiers and security personnel stopped us. We did not have the necessary Egyptian permits.

So now I am here at the northern border crossing, having taken a late-night flight from Cairo to Amman and a taxi the rest of the way here. I have valid papers from the Israeli army and a six-month visa that runs up to November. When I was here in June, I got through easily, but that time I was here with the UN, which had 'co-ordinated' or cleared the visit with the Israeli authorities. Their systems of checks are very thorough, and the application process to get in can take months, with very little certainty of success whether you are going through Egypt or Israel.

When I left Amman, in Jordan, at the crack of dawn, I first had to cross the King Hussein Bridge over the River Jordan, where the border post between Israel and Jordan is to be found. The crossing is also known as the Allenby Bridge. This is the only border

At the airport in Cairo with Mohammad and the PalMed group. We decide to try the Sinai–Rafah route by taxi.

crossing that Palestinians who live in the occupied West Bank are allowed to use to get in and out of their own country. They are not allowed to use the Israeli Ben Gurion International Airport in Tel Aviv.

I had been warned that I might not be let in by the Israelis, but a hundred-dollar VIP border pass with a special shuttle driver made the crossing surprisingly easy. The security and passport control were strict. Naturally, I did not lie; I told them that I was going back to Gaza to carry out medical work and showed them the Israeli stamps in my passport from my last entry at Erez. Once over the border, I met my Palestinian driver Abdallah, who drove me the approximately eighty miles through Israel to Erez.

The atmosphere at Erez is tense. The soldier in the guardhouse waves me forward after a few minutes. He recognises me, I think.

'Hello, are you on duty again today?' I try to adopt a friendly, cheerful tone.

'What will you be doing, why are you entering, who do you work for?' He rattles off the questions automatically, as if they were memorised like a multiplication table.

Back in Cairo, after being stopped in Sinai by Egyptian security police. I was well looked after, as always, by the Norwegian Ambassador, Tor Wennesland, and his wife, Åse Vikanes. I took a shower, was given a briefing and some food before taking the late flight to Amman.

'Medical work, I'm a doctor. Helping to treat the wounded. Humanitarian work, which there's a real need for, as you know. I'll be working at al-Shifa Hospital.'

I can hear the staccato rhythm of my answers, but I keep calm. It is quite an exercise in itself to keep my anger in check when I know that the military power keeping the Palestinians under occupation, and now bombing them again, also has unrestricted control of who should be 'allowed' to enter. I take a deep breath.

'Do you have any weapons with you?'

'No, absolutely not. Just a stethoscope. The stethoscope is my weapon.' I try out a playful tone. He smiles back. 'And I've got some medical equipment, some special anaesthetic needles and catheters.'

He stops listening, writes something on a piece of paper, puts my red passport on top and pushes it all back through a metal drawer.

'You can go ahead.' He nods towards the main building behind the large steel gates.

'Can I go?' I ask him in bewilderment.

'Yes, go. Now!' It sounds as if he might change his mind at any moment.

I take a quick look at the white form he has filled out. My name and numbers match up. Now I am almost in. The scrum of people wanting to get in or out is growing. I run over to my luggage, which consists of two small trolley bags and a carrier bag containing chocolate and sweets from the duty-free shop. The steel gate opens slowly and I scurry over towards the large terminal building. I made it through the second needle eye. Now the third and last one lies ahead: passport control and the labyrinth.

Throughout the Erez complex, the Israeli checkpoints are positioned physically above those being checked. The same applies to passport control. The lady behind the bullet-proof glass is wearing glasses and doing her knitting. She definitely recognises me.

'Hello again, I'm back. So nice to see you. Do you remember me? I asked you to put a stamp in my passport last time. Have a look here.'

I push my passport through the hatch and point out the stamps from my last time crossing the border in June. That time I had answered with a friendly 'of course' when she asked if she should stamp it. She remembers it, and I think that saves me time and questions today, as she can see that I am 'legitimate'.

'What are you going to do?'

'Medical work, al-Shifa Hospital. We've got to help the wounded, haven't we, after all?'

I think I see her nod, almost imperceptibly. She stamps my passport, gives it back and smiles.

'Thanks very much,' I say, almost shouting with relief.

I have made through the third and last needle eye! I will soon be in now.

I dash onwards, past a heavily laden TV cameraman, on through the intricate steel turnstiles, which only a contortionist can get through with luggage, follow the red painted stripe on the ground through the labyrinth of gateways until I eventually emerge onto the completely fenced-off strip of asphalt, over half a mile in length, that leads on to Gaza. The sweat is running off me in the burning sun, and I speed up to be sure that they will not stop me and bring me back.

A Palestinian tuk-tuk, a motorcycle with a small cart on the back, comes humming towards me.

'Dr. Mads! You're back! Welcome to Gaza! Welcome to the war, again.' The porter with the rickshaw recognises me instantly, and we kiss each other on the cheek three times, as is customary here.

'Kif hak, doctor? How's it going?'

'Tamãm, al-ḥamdu lillãh. I'm well, all

Seen from Gaza, the enormous Israeli terminal building at the border at Erez looks impenetrable. This terminal is the only point of entry or departure from occupied Gaza to Israel.

praise and thanks to God! *Kif inte, habibi?* How's it going with you, my friend?'

'*Al-ḥamdu lillāh tamām.* Get in, I'll drive you.'

I lift my bags up onto the trailer and we drive off with a roar. The border post on the Palestinian side is a humble office, called Hamsa-Hamsa, where passport details are recorded. Those who wish to leave Gaza have to wait here until the Israelis allow them to move over to their side of the border. Today's crowd is quite large and restless. Several journalists recognise me and want interviews.

'Not now,' I tell them. 'First I've got to get to al-Shifa.'

Since nobody really knew when or if I would get in, there is nobody waiting to meet me. I go over to the two or three parked yellow Palestinian taxis.

'Who can drive me to al-Shifa?'

'That's dangerous, *habibi*. What are you offering?'

'I'll pay whatever it costs.'

'200 shekels?'

'OK!'

During wartime, the prices of critical

The Israeli wall around Gaza is over six metres high. From inside, it looks like a prison.

activities go up tenfold. The taxi driver takes my bags, I get into the front seat, and we drive off at high speed along the dusty gravel road.

'They've bombed Arba-Arba, the whole passport control point has gone.'

He points to the right at what was, until last week, the brand-new border post, where the Hamas government had set up a new passport and customs office. I went through it just a week ago. Now it has been bombed to pieces.

At a table beneath an olive tree on the left side of the road sit three Palestinian men in civilian clothing. I give them my passport.

They take down the details with a biro. Open-air passport control.

'You are welcome, Dr. Mads,' says one of them, handing me back my passport.

They seem to want to bomb everything, I think to myself. All the infrastructure has to be destroyed. This is not a case of using proportional military means to defeat a military opponent. It is Palestinian society itself, its infrastructure and any trace of state-building, that they want to destroy.

We speed off along back roads and between bomb craters. The driver points to the left.

The Palestinian side of the border at Erez, where passport controls are carried out in two sheds. ▶

'It was a playground for children. Not any more, Dr. Mads!'

The little playground has been blown to pieces. Colourful climbing frames, a roundabout and some swings lie there as twisted metal skeletons.

I look out of the car window in disbelief, as I have done many times before. I am back in Gaza – God knows how many times I have been here – and I find myself left with the absurd feeling of watching the same gloomy film again and again, only to see it getting worse each time.

FACTS

GAZA'S POPULATION

- 1.8 million inhabitants
- 43.6% under 15 years of age
- 17.6 is the median age
- 60,000 births annually
- Nearly 50% unemployment (February 2015)
- 71.6% are refugees (February 2015)

SOURCES: WHO, 'Situation Report: Gaza Crisis', Issue 1, 10 July 2014; UNRWA, 'Gaza Situation Report 78', 5 February 2015; OCHA-oPt, 'Fragmented Lives: Humanitarian Overview 2014', March 2015; Palestinian Central Bureau of Statistics.

13. JULY

BACK AT AL-SHIFA

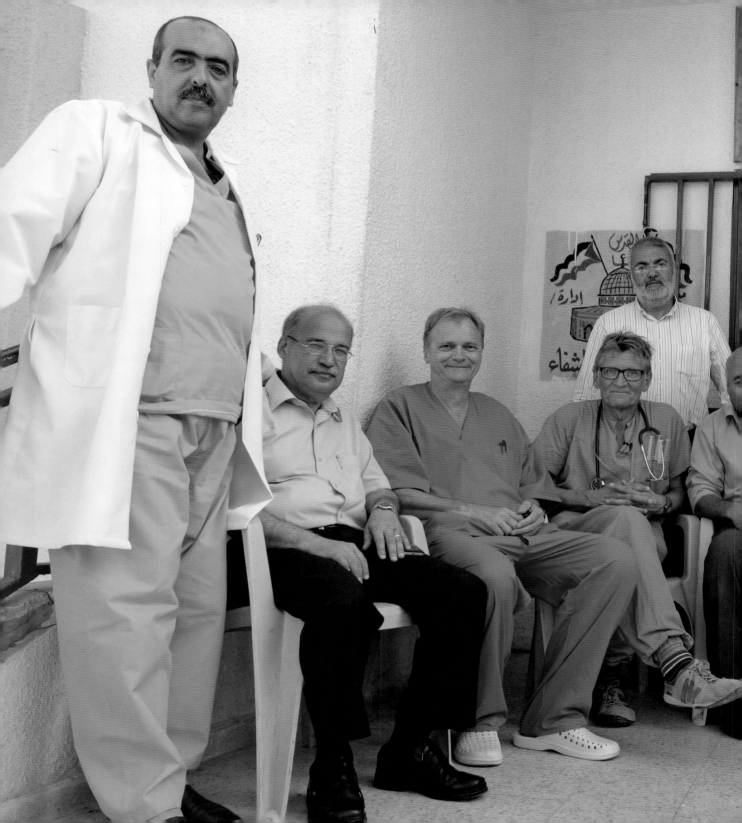

There was a warm and powerful reunion with Dr. Sobhi Skaik, Ashraf Mashharawi and Erik Fosse, who got in a few days before me. Dr. Mohammad is also on his way after he and his group got through Rafah, on the border with Egypt to the south.

The view towards the main entrance to al-Shifa Hospital. The sun is shining on the hospital mosque's minaret, rebuilt after it was ruined by Israeli bombing during Operation Cast Lead in 2008–09.

16.14

A heartfelt reunion with Dr. Issam, a surgeon and a close colleague of fifteen years' standing. We worked together at al-Shifa during the attack in 2009. On that occasion, his little nephew died on the operating table after being hit by a rocket from an Israeli drone. 'That's what our life is like, Mads, we've just got to keep going,' he said then. Now we are going through it again.

16.20

Dr. Mohammed al-Kashif, from the Ministry of Health, gives us a briefing on the situation. The crisis management team occupies this large room in the administration building. Meetings, intensive teamwork, food, prayer and sleep: everything happens here, twenty-four hours a day.

21.50 ▶

Dr. Sobhi Skaik holds an informal meeting with a group of doctors on a twelve-hour shift outside the emergency department. They discuss the organisation and share of responsibilities between the surgeons for that night. All of them are at work. None of them is getting paid.

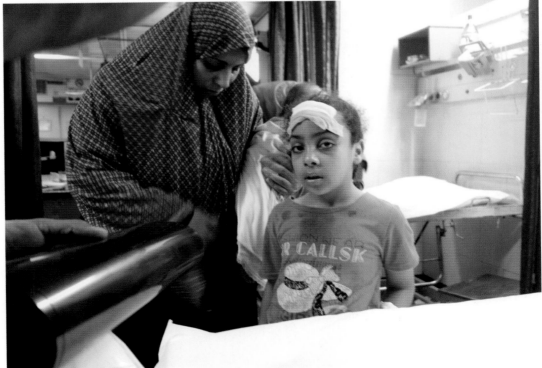

21.50 ▶

A family with children arrives at the emergency department after a bomb is dropped in the area. Small wounds. Cuts to the forehead. Blood on her pink T-shirt. She is checked over and sent back out. Out into the dark, with the sound of explosions around her.

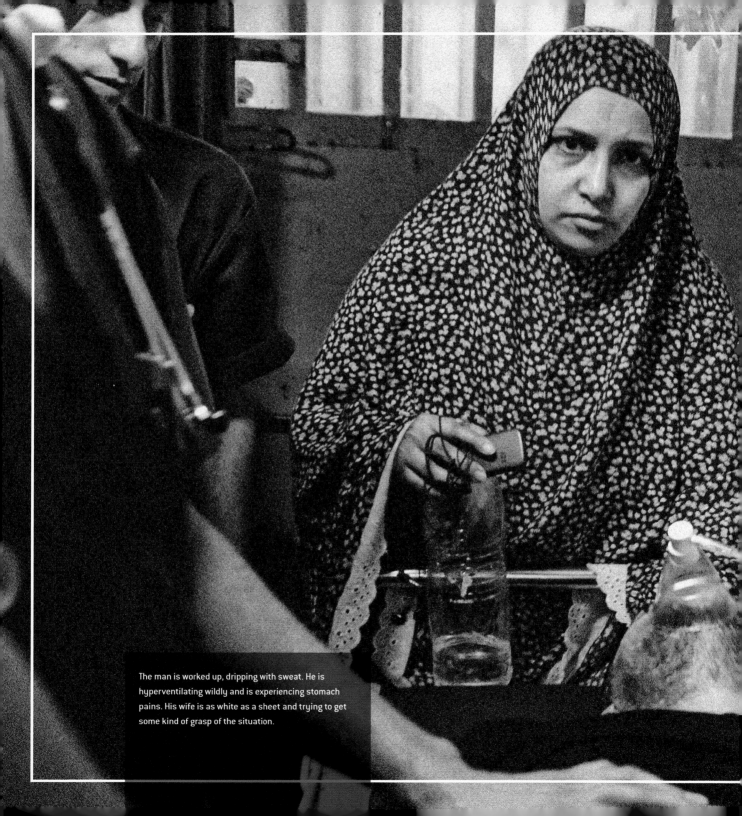

The man is worked up, dripping with sweat. He is hyperventilating wildly and is experiencing stomach pains. His wife is as white as a sheet and trying to get some kind of grasp of the situation.

16. JULY

NIGHT IN GAZA

◀ We run towards the entrance
   to meet the ambulances
   and casualties.

◀ 'A whole family bombed,' says
   Dr. Issam in his broken Swedish.
   'Many children.'

THE TIME IS ALMOST A QUARTER past two. We are exhausted. Night slowly drifts towards morning, and we start to look forward to *suhoor*, the simple early-morning meal served before sunrise as part of the fasting rituals of Ramadan. I have decided to fast together with my colleagues. Not because I am Muslim or religious, but out of respect for their customs and because it is important to understand how fasting affects the body's performance of those I am working with.

I try to keep some kind of routine, to find a rhythm around which I can structure the hours and the days. The two meals associated with Ramadan are like fixed pegs, clearly defined times that everybody participates in and looks forward to: not only because we are thirsty, hungry and worn out after about fifteen hours of hard slog with neither food nor drink. The sense of social fellowship formed when we meet for *iftar* in the evenings and for *suhoor* in the early hours of the morning is at least as important as food and drink. The gatherings are small oases of peace and community.

Now the emergency department is quiet, and we are chatting about the past twenty-four hours. It is nine days since the Israeli attacks started. Egypt's proposal for a ceasefire collapsed yesterday, only hours after the Israelis and Palestinians had agreed to it.

Suddenly, a blast shakes the whole building.

'That was close. Maybe in Rimal?' says one of the young doctors.

The ambulance sirens wail their collective, dissonant lament. More casualties coming, the sirens call. As if everybody did not already know. But they heighten our state of readiness in the emergency department, the sound of the sirens triggering our senses like Pavlovian creatures. We get up quickly, walk towards the reception area door, checking that we have what we need in our pockets, fishing out a new pair of disposable gloves, pulling them over our hands, alert and ready to make another effort. I can feel a painful knot in my stomach.

Dr. Issam Abu Ajwa, an experienced surgeon, is also working on tonight's shift. He is like a big brother to me. Our shared history goes back a long way. We first met here in Gaza during the intifada in 2000, when we worked together in mobile field hospitals.

Now Issam is older by fifteen years, one heart attack, four Israeli wars of aggression, one heart operation and many personal losses. Like the vast majority of Palestinian families in Gaza, he has lost a great deal. I will never forget when he came into the operating theatre in January 2009, following an Israeli drone attack, to confirm that the dying child on the operating table, with explosive injuries and amputated limbs, was his sister's son. We stopped our resuscitation attempts after Issam had confirmed his nephew's identity. I was crying, but Issam lifted my chin up, looked me straight in the eyes and said: 'That's what our life is like, Mads, we've just got to keep going.' Then he went back to the operating theatre next door and continued operating on another critically wounded patient.

Dr. Nafez is also on duty tonight, another old friend and colleague. Much younger, barely forty, but a consultant anaesthetist, married with five children. He is tremendously skilled but has no opportunity to develop further.

'We lack equipment for local and regional anaesthesia. We only have one kind of local anaesthetic. No nerve stimulator. We're short of everything, and that affects our options for safe and effective pain relief. We could've helped many people with epidurals, spinal blocks or nerve blocks. Now it's either a general anaesthetic or an inadequate local anaesthetic. The siege is so destructive for our medical work. We should at least have been allowed the equipment we need for all these injuries.'

Issam comes in from the ambulances, leading a small procession of wheeled stretchers.

'A whole family bombed,' he says in his broken Swedish, which he learnt during the years he spent as a surgeon in Sweden. 'Many children, but I think they'll be OK.'

The family of five come through the door behind him. The father and a boy of about nine each lie on their own trolley. The mother, in her mid-thirties, leads two daughters, the youngest aged six or seven, while the elder sister is around thirteen. All five of them are breathing and are awake. They are taken to the left, to the area for 'walking, talking wounded'. This is how the basic sorting, or triage, works: only those with clearly serious traumatic injuries, those who cannot speak or walk, are taken to the right, into the emergency department itself.

The father is very shaken and is the most severely affected. He is hyperventilating wildly and complaining of strong abdominal pain. His black T-shirt is soaked with sweat, which is running off his face. The children are a deathly pale white. The little girl and her big sister are put on a trolley bed, and Issam puts an oxygen mask on the little girl. The brother is put on the trolley next to them, and I examine him quickly. He is lying down, eyes closed. No visible signs of external injuries. He is awake, lucid and breathing quickly. The sound of his lungs breathing is fine when I listen to them. He smells like a warm child does. I ask him if it hurts anywhere. He shakes his head, his eyes still shut.

We turn him carefully onto his side. I pull up his white vest with blue stripes and the text 'Sport Super' written on it, so that I can examine his back. Carefully and systematically, I examine the back of his head, his ears, neck and back. I pull his pants down briefly to check if there are injuries on his bottom or if there is any blood coming from the rectum. Everything is OK. A quick check of his legs and arms. Nothing broken. I feel his stomach, which is soft and not sore to the touch. A 'top-to-toe' assessment like this does not take long but is important to avoid overlooking any injuries.

'What happened?' Dr. Issam asks in a loud and commanding voice.

The three children wait anxiously. ▶
Their mother is with them the
whole time, uninjured and caring,
but frightened.

The younger girl is given an ▶
oxygen mask, which Dr. Issam
then takes off. 'She'll be fine,'
he says.

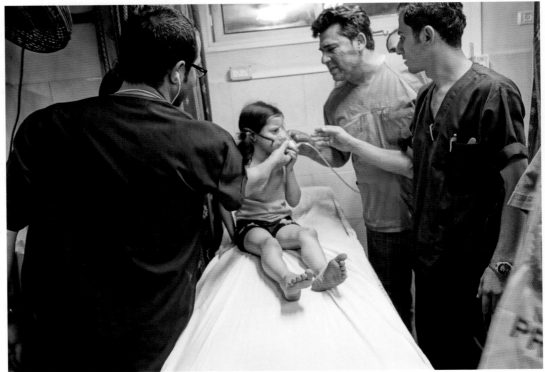

'Rockets. They shot rockets into our flat. We thought we were all going to die,' the woman answers quietly. Her husband speaks but is unintelligible behind the oxygen mask. Dr. Nafez has examined him and tells me quietly that he cannot find anything wrong.

'Shock- and stress-induced hyperventilation and stomach ache. Totally understandable,' he says.

The two girls stare with their large, dark eyes set against their pale faces. We cannot find anything wrong with them either and take the oxygen mask off the younger girl. Their mother is standing at the foot of the stretcher with a deeply concerned face. She is wearing a beautiful floor-length *chador*, dark blue with small floral patterns and pretty white lace edgings that come into view when she lifts her hands. Her face is as white as a sheet, like her husband's.

I use careful physical closeness and clear, honest information as key soothing agents when people have experienced shock and traumatic incidents. It has taken a few minutes, but now we have got the full picture. I speak to the two girls while holding their hands, eventually catching their gaze.

'It's going to be all right. Nobody's going to die. Dad's breathing heavily because he's a bit scared, just like you. Your brother and your mum are fine. Are you frightened?'

The little one shakes her head enthusiastically and smiles a little, clearly relieved. Her elder sister looks at me solemnly with her dark eyes. She nods.

43

'Yes,' she whispers, barely audible.

We get their father to sit up and I inform both the parents that we have not found anything wrong.

'*Al-ḥamdu lillāh*, all praise and thanks to God,' the mother answered.

'But what happened? Are you able to tell me?' I ask them.

The father is feeling better. He is breathing more calmly and gets up from his stretcher, while the mother gently embraces her children. I lead them over to an empty bed on the other side of the room, so the three bed-spaces can be freed up for other casualties coming in.

'We were in our flat, which is on the third floor, not far away from here in the middle of Gaza City. It's a dual-aspect flat, and we normally stay with Grandma. First came a rocket that didn't detonate. We ran for our lives across the corridor and to the other side of the building. Then came another rocket that blew up our entire flat. Smashed it to pieces. We couldn't take anything, we just fled.'

The time is almost three o' clock in the morning now. The children are in their pyjamas, while the parents had not yet gone to bed when the explosion took place.

'I was sure that we were going to be killed, that it was the end. Terrible. Terrible,' says the father. He holds his three children tightly and smiles.

The three children lean on him, the four of them together forming their own little universe of unity and safety. The mother is making calls from her mobile to tell the rest of the family that everybody is alive and well. For the moment.

'*Al-ḥamdu lillāh!*'

In the space of forty-three minutes, this small family has gone from being fragmented, fearful of imminent death and filled with massive uncertainty to a family coming together, regaining their strength and rebuilding their own little social network. Their house has been destroyed, but they are alive. They have each other.

FACTS

GAZA'S INTERNAL REFUGEES

OCHA-oPt estimates that c. 500,000 Palestinians, 28% of the population, were internally displaced during the attacks on Gaza in July and August 2014.

- 239,000 were in emergency shelters at UN schools
- 49,000 were accommodated in government school buildings
- 170,000 in empty buildings, churches, mosques or with host families

As of late December 2014, an estimated 100,000 remained homeless. Some were renting temporary accommodation, while others were still in communal accommodation or with host families. Others spent the winter in prefabricated units, tents, makeshift shelters, or camping out in the ruins of their homes.

SOURCE: OCHA-oPt, 'Fragmented Lives: Humanitarian Overview 2014', March 2015; OCHA-oPt, 'Gaza: Initial Rapid Assessment', 27 August 2014; Shelter Cluster Palestine, 'Shelter Cluster Factsheet', March 2015.

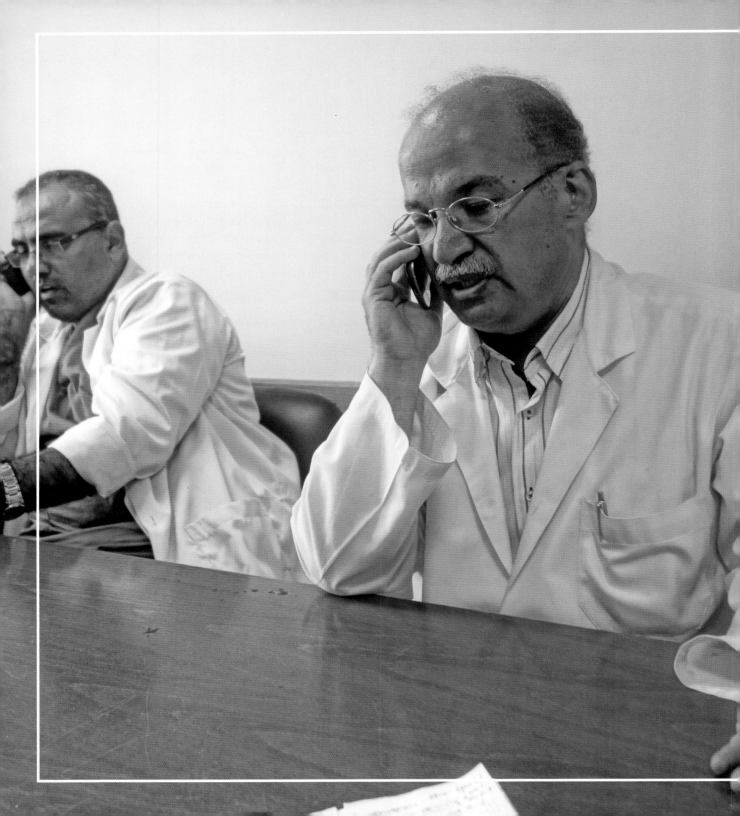

PEOPLE OF GAZA:
DR. SOBHI SKAIK

HE HOLDS OUT HIS HAND IN a gesture of despondency, while maintaining his calm. The voice at the other end of the call on his mobile was clearly asking him yet another foolish question.

'The point is that the people of Gaza are being killed. They have no place to shelter. The wounded have nowhere to go. Besides, if you look at the World Health Organisation's definitions of illness and health, it's not just a case of treating disease or injuries: you have to take care of people's social and economic wellbeing too, so they can survive. And what about a wounded person who comes to our hospital for treatment now: where can they go if we discharge them? Where will they fit in? How will they live? This is a major problem now.'

Dr. Sobhi points a cautionary finger to underline the point, as if lecturing to his students, before going on.

'It's not as simple as us just carrying out an operation and then saying: "Go home!"' He clicks his fingers for emphasis. 'They don't even have homes any more. There's no money to buy food for... Yes?'

The journalist at the other end interrupts him. He listens. Impatiently. His leg starts shaking a little, but he keeps a straight face, answering amiably and with authority, in his British-sounding accent.

'Yes. No. No. As simple as that! If they attack our hospital, how will we protect ourselves? Our patients? What can we do?'

He shrugs again in resignation.

'Yes, of course. We would try to solve the problem, yes, maybe with tents. But we haven't got the tents at our disposal, and the hospital can't act as a shelter, or we wouldn't be able to do our jobs. It wouldn't be safe for them either.'

His oval, polished glasses with thin golden mounts frame his sharp expression, his upper lip adorned with a distinguished grey moustache. His white doctor's coat is spotless and freshly ironed, and he is wearing a blue-striped white open-neck shirt. He could have been a consultant surgeon starting his day at a well-resourced clinic in London or Oslo, taking a call from a journalist. But the scene this morning, on Thursday 24 July 2014, is less like a peaceful hospital in well-fed cities just a short flight away, and more like hell on earth. There is a war going on.

We are having an emergency meeting in the surgical department with the rest of the management team. Dr. Sobhi is the medical director of the whole hospital, with hundreds of tasks to handle. For twenty years, in his roles as a surgeon and a manager, he has been developing surgical facilities for the population of Gaza. He has put in place a recognised programme of specialist training for surgeons based on a European-style model, introduced systematic procedures for the treatment of injuries at al-Shifa and, four years ago, he started kidney transplantation in Gaza, which has already helped fourteen patients, between the wars.

He keeps on listening patiently to the torrent of words from the journalist.

'In any case, the situation is dreadful and we have no idea whether or not they'll attack us. It's a real mess. And the hospitals in Gaza are clearly not immune.'

More questions. The journalist is not giving up yet.

'No. This is a hospital for patients. I don't see any political leaders here. No, nobody's hiding here. This hospital is here to treat patients, and that's what we do. Day and night. We're overcrowded everywhere, in every department. It would be untrue to say any other activity is going on at the hospital. We treat all the wounded who come in, whether they're civilians, militants or Israelis. That's our Hippocratic oath, it's as simple as that. And we follow it, but we're drowning in refugees and patients, and there's nothing to help us. Our stores are empty. Every kind of equipment and medicine is in short supply; we already had shortages before this latest act of aggression.'

The discussion comes to an end, and he patiently spells out his e-mail address to the journalist. Then his voice becomes louder: 'Let me add one last thing. I appeal to the international community to care more about Gaza. The people of Gaza are being killed in a brutally terrorising fashion. I don't know what terrorism means any more, but this is definitely terror. Stop the killing in Gaza! They can't let this carry on.'

The same courteous dignity and an almost obstinate sense of discipline shine through in everything he undertakes. Again and again, day after day. He stands there through attack after attack, as steady as a rock, like a ship's captain in a storm. A small man with enormous responsibility.

He can be seen there at any time, day or night. Listening observantly and with care, but also staying clear, sharp and determined, with an intense energy in his role as the head of management. He always gets people to follow him, calming conflicts, cleaning up, showing the way forward through chaos when the rest of us lose hope.

I have known him for fifteen years and seen him lead al-Shifa Hospital through four wars. He is undoubtedly one of the world's most experienced war surgeons and disaster managers. When I ask him what are the three most important principles guiding him in managing the hospital, he answers without hesitation:

'Whatever we do, we must always stay focused on our patients and on caring for them humanely. Then we must secure treatment for our patients according to their needs and our resources, and we must get the experts the equipment and resources they need to do their job. These are the three most important things.'

'And Gaza, what does it mean to you?'

'Gaza is the paradise of God on earth. Gaza is a part of Palestine, and Palestine is our country. We are part of Palestine, and Palestine is part of us.'

16. JULY

THE LADS ON THE BEACH

'THEY'VE DAMAGED 16,000 HOUSES SO FAR! 1100 houses are completely destroyed! How will we manage to reconstruct them if they won't open the borders?'

Sweat runs down his face while he continues speaking with growing intensity. His hands gesticulate rhythmically in time with short sentences spoken in his unmistakeable New York accent: an unbroken monologue, with words delivered like machine-gun fire.

'This isn't civilised. This is inhumane. We're people, not animals, we're Palestinians! We're highly educated and we want peace. We're searching for peace. We want peace today, or tomorrow. We want a ceasefire, but not a ceasefire that kills us. They have to open the borders. We must have a ceasefire that opens up our people's lives. We don't want to live confined like animals with no rights. We want a peaceful life, but look what they're doing to our children, our women, to everybody. They're killing us. What kind of world is it we live in? What kind? I ask you journalists and I ask the world. What kind of world? Why are we being treated like this?'

His bodyguard discreetly passes him a tissue. He mops his brow. The new Palestinian Minister of Public Works, Mofeed al-Hasayneh, is a short, suited man with a blue tie and a small, neat moustache. He spent over twenty years living in the United States. In June, he was appointed Minister of Public Works and Housing in the new Palestinian unity government formed by Fatah and Hamas. Finally, the Palestinians had a joint government to represent both the West Bank and Gaza. Mofeed al-Hasayneh is one of the few in the government to represent Gaza, and now he is visiting hospital patients for the first time as minister.

Three boys of about ten are sitting on their hospital beds, looking alarmed at the sight of the man losing his temper in front of them. There has been a constant stream of press and family visiting them, but Mofeed al-Hasayneh is making probably the first ministerial visit. Yesterday, the lads were at the beach. They were playing football and hide-and-seek when the attack came. Four of their best friends were killed.

I walk cautiously over to the boys and whisper to them that the minister is not angry with them, but with the people who shot at them. They nod, but remain silent.

'Where's the humanity?' The minister points at the three wounded, bandaged, young boys in their beds.

'When I lived in New York, I saw no sympathy for our people, not even when they killed our children. Why aren't we allowed to organise ourselves? Do they think we're wild animals living in the jungle? There have been four wars now, and they've tried to kill the name of Palestine, not only its people. We're

'The beach was our best playground.'

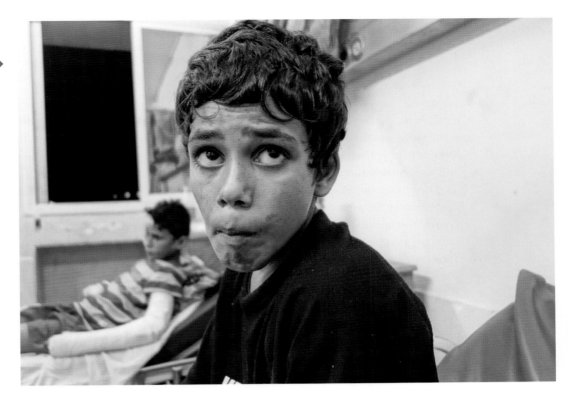

The family gathers around Motasem (11). 'We used to play on the beach and go fishing together. I don't know what we'll do now.' ▶

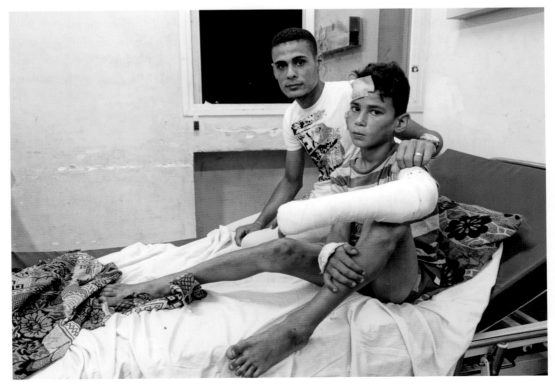

asking for Gaza's borders to be opened, for trucks with food and goods to be let in. Let us sell our goods to the outside world. Allow us to live our lives with dignity! Then the ceasefire will be permanent. A peaceful solution.'

Then he has to take a break. The crowd of journalists in the cramped hospital room has listened and taken notes. It is not every day they get to interview a Palestinian minister in Gaza. The camera crews step back while the minister and his entourage move towards the door.

The four lads who were killed came to al-Shifa yesterday, lifeless and beyond hope. Their families came streaming when the bodies were carried out of the emergency department, spontaneously following them to the mortuary round the back. Shouts of rage filled the whole area around the hospital. The boys' small bodies lay on large orange ambulance stretchers, which were lifted high above people's heads, the bodies shifting limply from side to side in time with the continuous steps of the bearers below. I looked on in shock at the large crowd of grieving and angry men as they passed the media tent in front of the main entrance.

'But wasn't there a ceasefire?' I wondered out loud.

'We can never trust a ceasefire.' The answer came from a doctor just behind me, who was also following the dramatic scene.

The three young boys who were wounded managed to drag themselves over to the al-Deira Hotel, next to the beach, where the foreign journalists are staying. Harald Henden, a photo-journalist for the Norwegian newspaper *VG*, was close by when the shells exploded. He made a valiant and determined effort to administer first aid to the boys and get them transported to al-Shifa. Harald was still upset and shaken by the incident when we spoke by the boys' hospital beds.

The attack took place at the popular sandy beach by Gaza City's fishing harbour, a few blocks down from al-Shifa Hospital. The group of boys belonged to the Bakr family, who are mainly fishermen and, in terms of politics, belong to Fatah. The four lads who were killed were cousins and were clearly neither 'militia' nor 'terrorists'. Israeli gunboats or aircraft fired a shell that killed the first of the four boys. A second shell hit the other three, desperately fleeing across the beach, trying to reach safety. The four who were killed were Ahed Atef Bakr and Zakaria Ahed Bakr, each ten years old, the eleven-year-old Mohammed Ramiz Bakr, and nine-year-old Ismail Mohammed Bakr.

The three survivors at al-Shifa suffered minor injuries, although broken bones and abdominal shrapnel wounds requiring emergency life-saving surgery can hardly be called minor injuries for children who were playing.

When I return to the three boys at around eight o'clock in the evening, the mood is lighter. The room is full of relatives of every age, and the three boys are calm, but still solemn.

'We've got nobody to play with now. They fired four rockets. The first two killed our friends, the third wounded us, and the fourth tore off the leg of a man who came to help us.'

The boy talking looks straight at me with his intensely questioning eyes. Is he searching for answers?

'They shot at us even though they knew we were children playing football on the beach,' says the eleven-year-old Motasem, sitting up in the bed closest to the window, facing the sea. He sits there, wearing only his underpants and a striped cotton shirt, surrounded by slightly older relatives with their arms carefully around him. His left arm is in a long plaster cast, and he has two bandages over his right eye and cheek. His expression is one of utter dejection and deep seriousness, his mouth clenched.

'The fighters were away at the front anyway, fighting the Israelis; they weren't playing football on the beach.' He sighs. 'It was probably an Israeli officer who didn't like us playing football.'

The other two are silent. They both look at me with the same sombre expression.

I give them some small presents I have brought from Norway. Some good-quality drawing materials, some sweets and stickers. It feels so little. They take them, hesitantly, glancing at their older relatives, who nod back. We carry on talking, but their English vocabulary is not that extensive, just like my Arabic.

I say good night, ruffle the boys' hair, look them in the eyes and wish them peace – *ma salaam* – as I take my leave.

On my way down the stairs, I feel a gnawing disquiet. Would there have been as much attention paid to this incident had it not happened in front of the eyes of the entire international press corps at the al-Deira Hotel? How many similar cases of infanticide are *not* covered?

Even worse, what would have been the world's reaction if Palestinian soldiers had killed four young Israeli boys playing football on a beach in Tel Aviv? The uncomfortable answer is a simple one: the world would have been shouting about terrorism more loudly than ever. Why is it not terrorism when Israel does it?

Of course it is terrorism. State terrorism.

FACTS

ISRAELI LOSSES

According to Israeli official figures, 73 Israelis were killed. Among this number were:

- 67 soldiers
- 6 civilians, including one child and one migrant worker

469 Israeli soldiers and 255 Israeli civilians were wounded.

SOURCE: Bachmann et al. (2015) 'Gaza, 2014: Findings of an Independent Medical Fact-Finding Mission'.

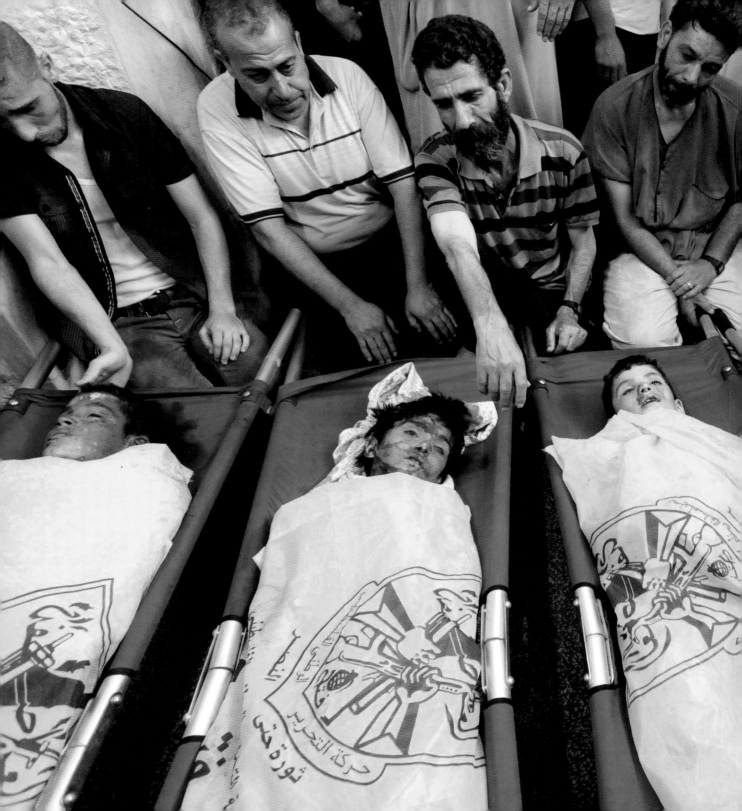

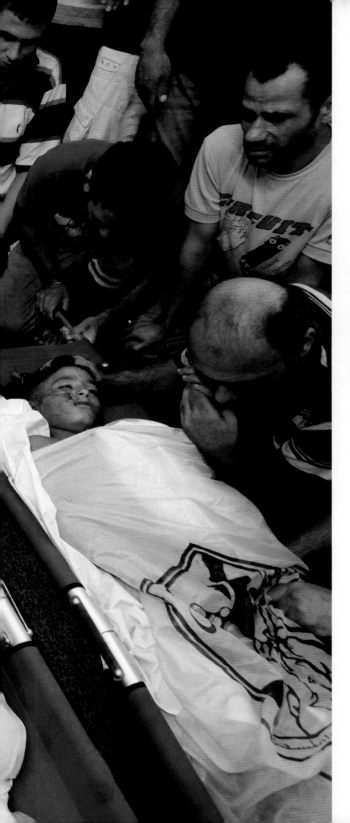

◄ The four boys who were killed while playing football:
Ahed Atef Bakr and Zakaria Ahed Bakr, each ten years
old, Mohammed Ramiz Bakr, aged eleven, and Ismail
Mohammed Bakr, nine years old. They are all draped in
the yellow flag of Fatah, while bereaved family members
pay their respects at the burial.

The despairing father of one of the four young boys
who were killed.

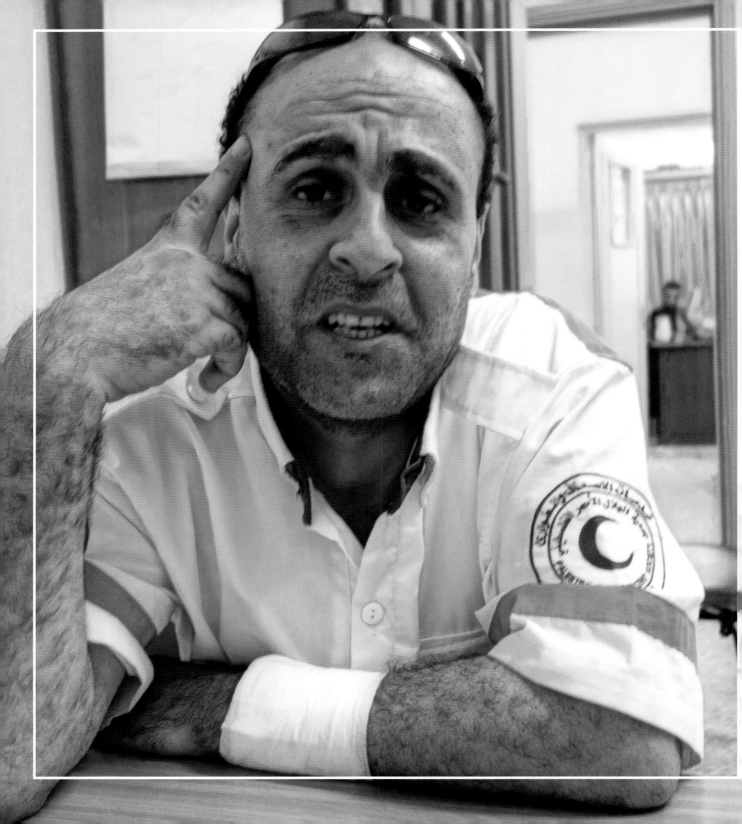

PEOPLE OF GAZA:
AYMAN THE AMBULANCE WORKER

'SHE PHONES ME ALMOST EVERY FIVE minutes. You must remember that we live in Khan Younis, about twenty miles south of here towards Rafah, and I don't have the chance to go home that often in between shifts. It's far too dangerous. Not a single square inch is safe when the Israelis attack. Besides, our shifts are endless, but what can we do?'

Ayman has been working in the ambulance service for seventeen years, and has worked all that time in Gaza. Since he was a child, his dream was to be a paramedic. Now the nightmares come one after another. Both he and his wife had a terrible time during this most recent attack.

'It's difficult to get to sleep. I keep on waking up, and when I do get to sleep, I have bad dreams. It's probably normal, but I get so tired,' he says.

He looks pale and weary, with black stubble on his face.

'And I see so many things,' he adds, almost to himself.

We are sitting on the stairs leading up to the administration building. It is nighttime. Everything beyond the light of the hospital is blacked out, which only heightens the eerie feeling. The threatening thunder of the bombing to the east does not distract us, but it can be heard. Ayman turns towards me.

'This is the worst I've ever experienced, Dr. Mads. It's by far the dirtiest war they've carried out. You can't imagine the things we see out there,' he says, nodding in the direction of the blasts. 'And we've never, ever had so many women and children among the casualties. We can't get to many places or reach everywhere when the raids happen. They've killed so many people.'

His white ambulance uniform is creased and dripping with sweat after a tough shift. Embroidered on each sleeve of the uniform is the emblem of the Red Crescent. This symbol should protect him, his workmate, their patient and their ambulance under international law, but that is not how it works in Gaza. A number of ambulance workers have already been wounded or killed in active service. Many more will follow before the attacks are over.

'When their attacks don't hit the militia, they turn their weapons against the civilian population. I hope nobody else ever sees what I've seen.' He looks at me, his face serious. 'You need to be careful too: stay here at al-Shifa.'

A few months later, the war is over. A ceasefire, the international donors' conference, hopes and promises. Gaza slips out of the media's focus, with Ebola and IS taking the place of Israel and Gaza. I reach Ayman via Skype from Tromsø. He is on duty at the ambulance station in Gaza City, and we greet each other warmly over the slightly flickering screen.

'Before you say anything, Mads, I just have to say thank you to the Norwegian people. We feel that you're supporting us, and we need that. Everybody here loves Norway, don't forget that.'

'But how's it going?'

'We're not sleeping well, most of us. I have nightmares, waking up screaming and scaring my wife. Haven't got the energy to talk to anybody.'

'How's she doing?'

'Not so well. The house next door was bombed to pieces while I was on duty. All the windows in our house were blown out. She was naturally terrified and ran out into the street. I had to send a local ambulance to help her. The children aren't too bad, but we're under a huge amount of pressure. The siege hasn't lifted in the slightest since the ceasefire. I see a lot of mental illness among the patients we pick up. Everybody's struggling.'

Ayman laughs on the screen in front of me: 'We had a kind of group session with some therapists from Italy who gave us a stress ball to squeeze. I think our experiences were a bit too much for them to handle, so I told them maybe I should help *them*...'

'But Ayman, why don't you leave? You've got three children, you're stressed and you have to spend a lot of time away from your wife, who's not well.'

He turns serious again. 'I don't want to leave Gaza. This is my country. I want to die in my own country. But I want to have peace, get the borders opened, travel like normal people do and go to visit my family on the West Bank. I want a life.'

> **FACTS**
>
> During the 51 days of the Israeli attack, between 21 and 23 health workers were killed, and 83 injured, most of whom were ambulance workers. 16 ambulances were damaged or totally destroyed.
>
> **SOURCES:** OCHA-oPt, 'Gaza Strip: Damaged Clinics as of 5 Sept. 2014'. Health Cluster in the occupied Palestinian territory, 'Gaza Strip Joint Health Sector Assessment Report', September 2014.

Ayman took care of us too, bringing us gifts in the middle of so much turmoil: a gift for his friend Merete Taksdal, a faithful activist for the Palestinian cause in Norway, and a new ambulance vest for me. 'Remember that this vest is a token of respect from us in the ambulances.'

THE TIME IS PAST FOUR IN the morning when I finally stagger off to the hotel for a few hours' sleep. I feel utterly exhausted. The day has taken its toll. Countless patients have been admitted, maybe about a hundred. The living and the dying, the injured and the uninjured.

Some situations and patients were especially painful sights and are still burnt in my mind, like when you have been looking straight at the sun and then close your eyes tight, a retinal imprint. In the deep labyrinths of the human memory, however, the imprint stays forever.

I walk out of the hospital gates, look down the empty street and glance up at the pitch-black sky to see if I can spot the drone buzzing above my head. For them, up there, we are so infinitely small down here. They can see everything, monitoring every movement, tapping every call, and reading every text message or letter. They also have a monopoly on air and sea power. Their F-16 fighter-bombers meet no opposition, flying freely and bombing wherever they wish. The same goes for their drones and Apache helicopters. The Palestinians have no air force, no effective anti-aircraft defences or early warning systems with sirens to alert the civilian population. Neither do they have bomb shelters or advanced missile shields against incoming Israeli attacks.

1.7 million Palestinians are denied the right to flee the bombing, because Israel and the United States, with the tacit support of countries such as Norway, have closed all the emergency exits, blocked all escape routes and sealed Gaza on land, at sea and in the air. Those responsible for the bombing have trapped their victims, mercilessly.

The sound of the drone grows louder as I walk towards the hotel. The street is deserted, without a single car or a single person. Normally, there is heavy traffic here both day and night.

At the corner I am approaching, there is a taxi rank for people heading to the south of Gaza, a bustling transport node, but now it is deserted too. The drone makes a shrill sound; the frequency is getting higher. Is it coming closer? Are they aiming at me? I quicken my pace instinctively. If I hold my breath for the last thirty steps, everything will be fine. Magical thinking, whatever it takes. I am afraid.

I have seen so many shattered, torn and shot people over the past day that the thought of my own vulnerability hits close to home. I can feel it in my stomach. After all, I am just as vulnerable myself. The health workers like me wear our green hospital scrubs indoors and out. No helmets, no bullet-proof vests like those worn by many of the foreign reporters who visit al-Shifa. Nothing. We are just as exposed as all the civilian patients who flock to the hospital.

The fear is tangible. A feeling of being confronted by a force so cynical and powerful that nobody is safe. After all, the Israelis have killed at least 230 people and wounded over 1700 in only ten days, mainly civilians, including health workers.

The large wrought iron gate at the entrance to Marna House is locked, with no way to open it. I quickly shine the head torch I am holding, letting out only a small strip of light through my fingers in order not to be spotted. Closed. Right, I don't want to wake the watchmen, who have finally got a chance to catch some sleep in there, so I climb over. The gate might be over eight feet tall, but it has smart wrought iron patterns well-suited for climbing. 'Easy now,' I say to myself. 'Don't get stuck.' Imagine if my foot became stuck as I jumped down and I ended up breaking a leg. Guests easily become a burden in wartime.

Once through the door of the empty reception, I can finally breathe normally again. I pick up my key, shine my way up the narrow marble stairs to the first floor and find my door, which is waiting for me wide open. In order to diminish the effect of the pressure waves of the bombs, all the doors and windows are open. They know what they are doing here: the Palestinians know all the simple precautions to take. During the attacks in 2009, all the windows and glass doors in the hotel were smashed by the bombing around al-Shifa, making the place uninhabitable. They know it could happen again.

I glance quickly at the room's wall-mounted television set. The small, red standby light is not on. All right, so there is no electricity, not that it really matters. I would probably not have turned on the light anyway.

I systematically empty the pockets of my green operating smock, taking out my syringes, torch, camera, three mobile phones, my small black Moleskine notebook with the elastic around it, and the folded piece of paper with the print-out from the Ministry of Health of the casualty summary for the last few days.

My smock is damp and sticky, and it smells of blood as I pull it off, over my head. When I untie my belt, my green trousers barely stay hanging on around my waist.

I hang up my clothes neatly to air on a hanger before sitting down heavily on the edge of the bed. Only the sounds of the drone and some distant explosions can be heard; otherwise the night is still.

Then the images come back to me. Some I have captured forever with my camera lens, while others are a nebulous wave of sounds, smells, and that strange feeling of touching shattered bodies. I am ready to collapse from exhaustion, but I cannot face the thought of lying down to sleep. The experiences of the past day and night are still writhing about inside me. My computer battery is still charged. I take off my camera's black leather case, turn it round and take out the memory card, sliding it into the opening on the left-hand side of the laptop and starting the automatic download. Routine and discipline. The photographs must not be lost. I have a quick scan through some of the patients we have treated. The pictures bring short

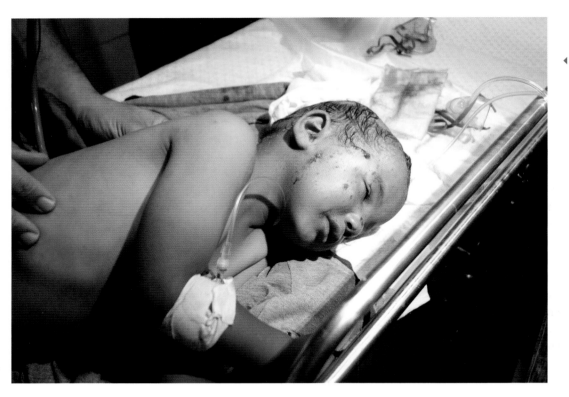

A three-year-old boy with splinter wounds to the upper body and the face. He is awake and terribly frightened. We have to carry out a quick ultrasound scan of the boy's chest and abdominal cavity to rule out internal bleeding. He screams in fear and pain. I try to comfort him with some gentle words, a few of which in Arabic. The language used does not matter so much. A voice means somebody is there, and you are not alone. Anybody can offer that and a friendly hand. It helps, and he calms down. No haemorrhaging. His wounds are cleaned, but he cannot stay in hospital, due to the overcrowding. Tough decisions have to be made.

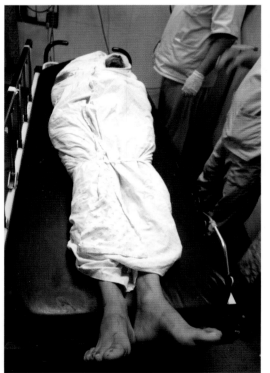

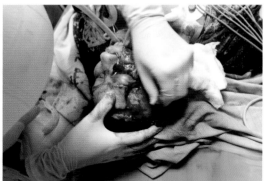

23.30

A young man with critical explosive injuries. Unconscious and dying. We intubate him, inserting two thoracic drains into his chest cavity at the same time, one on each side. Major bleeding on both sides. No response, no blood pressure, no pulse. We agree to stop. There is a consensus. I disconnect the bag valve mask, cutting off the blood-stained tape stuck to his neck to keep the plastic airway tube steady. His nose is partially blown off. He is quickly wrapped up in a white sheet that is a little too short, leaving his feet jutting out.

21.30

A pregnant woman has been hit in the face by shrapnel. The splinter has practically sliced off the right half of her face, in a vertical line from the hairline down past her right eye, which has been spared, in beneath her eyelid towards the bridge of her nose past the right corner of her mouth and down to her jaw. We worked well as a team treating her when she came to the emergency department at about half past nine. She was breathing, conscious and was bleeding heavily from the wounds to her face and mouth. Her injuries were bad, but they were survivable. A quick examination revealed no other lethal wounds. We administered an emergency anaesthetic, struggling with her airway but succeeding at the third attempt. Her left eye closed, but her right eye stared out vacantly into the room. Having been sent quickly to the operating theatre, she can make it.

episodes back to my mind, episodes already destined for the secure vault where our most painful memories are stored. I stay sitting on the edge of the bed.

Do people in the world out there really know what is happening? Can they see the damage, the pain and the scale of loss, a story that cannot be conveyed by the cold statistics? Can people around the world, not least people in power, see the impact these heavy attacks are having, with the bombs, the missiles launched from drones, and now artillery fire? Does anybody out there feel outraged? Anybody with influence?

The sounds of the bombing have intensified again.

I must write. I must write to those who are not here, who cannot see what is happening with their own eyes.

Writing usually helps when I have nobody to speak with. The pictures have finished downloading. Now I want to download my thoughts and feelings at this very moment. I choose to write in English, maybe because I want to write to friends in the United States who I know are following events carefully. The words flow quickly over the keyboard:

Dearest friends,
The last night was extreme. The 'ground invasion' of Gaza resulted in scores and carloads with maimed, torn apart, bleeding, shivering, dying... All sorts of injured Palestinians, all ages, all civilians, all innocent.

The heroes in the ambulances and in all of Gaza's hospitals are working 12 to 24-hour shifts, grey from fatigue and inhuman workloads (without payment [at] all in Shifa for the last four months). They care, triage, try to understand the incomprehensible chaos of bodies, sizes, limbs, walking, not walking, breathing, not breathing, bleeding, not bleeding humans. Humans!

Midway through the letter, I address President Obama directly:

Mr Obama – do you have a heart? I invite you – spend one night – just one night – with us in Shifa. Disguised as a cleaner, maybe. I am convinced, 100 per cent, it would change history.

It takes me no more than a few minutes to write the letter. I cry as I write the words, my first tears since I arrived in this war, and they are not a moment before time.

The power is still down. I want to send it straight away, but that proves impossible.

'Just sleep on it.' An inner voice gives me some good advice. Maybe it comes from me, or maybe from some of the people I am with, constantly offering care and friendly guidance.

I save the letter, close the computer and brush my teeth in the dark. Simple routines can save us from descending into chaos or a breakdown. I grope my way to the bed, check that my mobile phones and torch are there on the bedside table, that my laces are untied and my shoes ready to be put on at a moment's notice. I pull up the cool sheet and fall asleep.

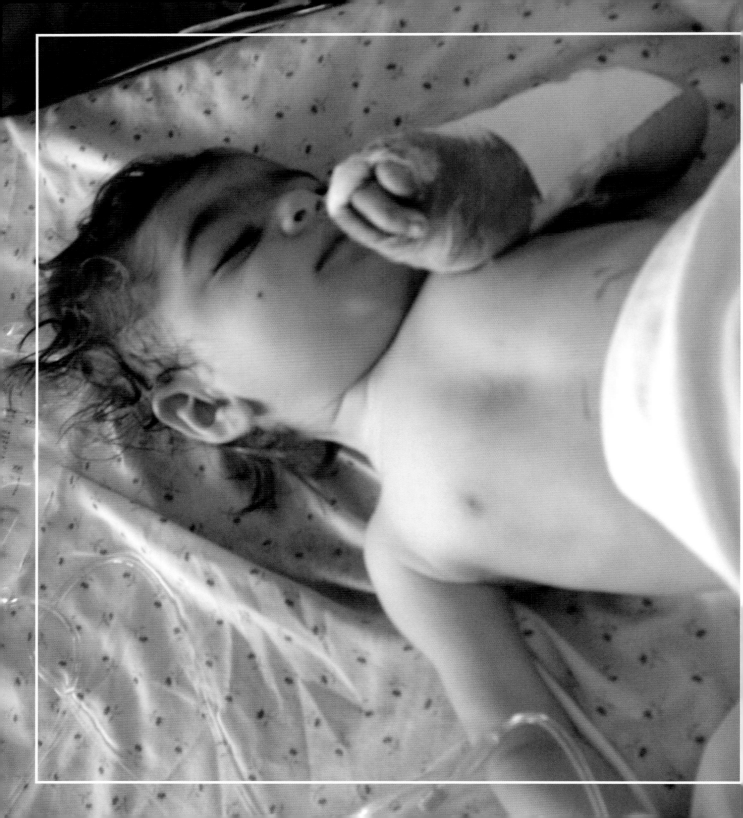

PEOPLE OF GAZA:
JUMANA

JUNE 2014. I AM VISITING JUMANA al-Samouni and her mother Meysa at their home. Every time I am in Gaza, I visit a number of the families I helped to treat during the 2009 war, in order to follow up on them, to help, and to learn.

When the atrocity happened on 4 January 2009, Jumana was still a baby, and Meysa was only nineteen years old. A fierce Israeli assault on Gaza was in full swing, another assault leading to major civilian casualties.

Meysa's husband was killed in January 2009, when Israeli ground forces herded together around a hundred members of the Samouni family in a warehouse in al-Zaytoun, just outside Gaza City. Then the Israelis bombed the building. Jumana's left hand was torn apart, almost thirty other relatives were killed and even more wounded.

After the massacre, the seriously injured Jumana, only nine months old, came to al-Shifa. Most of her tiny left hand had to be amputated. I remember well how only her delicate little finger and ring finger stuck out of the blood-stained bandage as I went to see to her after her anaesthesia.

My regular visits to see Jumana, her mother Meysa and the rest of the family have given me a deeper insight into the daily life of the Palestinians under the occupation and siege. The children of Gaza experience the fear and terrifying impact on the senses left by war, with the destruction of their neighbourhoods and their safety. A great number of children in Gaza also lose their closest relatives, parents,

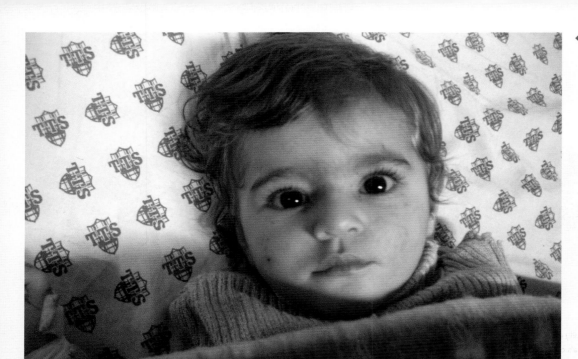

brothers and sisters, as well losing their own health, but that is not all. In between the regular Israeli attacks, the Palestinians' daily lives are constantly filled with anxiety as a result of the blockade. They have shortages of food and water, electricity, everyday goods and, not least, paid employment. Everything is difficult.

Nevertheless, Jumana has grown, in spite of the adversities and losses she has gone through. Her left hand still only has the little finger and ring finger, but she is strong and resourceful. She is good at catching and grasping things. Following her development has been a truly enlightening experience, as well as an example of children's flexibility, strength and ability to survive even the most traumatic losses and disasters.

Even though Meysa was widowed when she was only nineteen years old, she has been a wise and dependable mother to Jumana, with the crucial and close support of her family. Family is the absolute keystone of Palestinian culture and everyday life. For most people, a strong faith in God and the dream of one day being able to live as free men and women in their own country are also important factors in surviving all their hardships.

Jumana will soon be six years old and is looking forward to starting school. Her mother has remarried, and Jumana has a kind and caring new father.

Having compassionate parents and close

Meysa and Jumana in al-Zaytoun. 'What will the future bring for us? How will we cope? I'm a widow, only nineteen years old, with a disabled child. Can anybody fix Jumana's amputated fingers?'

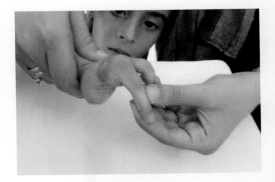

Meysa carefully opens Jumana's injured hand, while Jumana's cousin Amal watches on.

family ties with caring adults, who can identify and support a child's needs, coupled with the child's own ability to speak about their experiences, all serve to boost a child's power to survive extreme life-changing events. Gaza has over a million children and young people. Many of them have lost a lot, all of them have experienced bombing and death, while tens of thousands have lost their homes, schools and nurseries. Yet they endure it, and not only that: they grow.

Life is constantly winning small victories for a people who have been living through occupation, oppression, military dictatorship and death for almost seventy years. None of it is over yet.

Jumana is playful and secure, happily seeking contact with others. In November 2012 she experiences her second war.

'The ceasefire came three days ago, after eight days of bombing,' says Meysa. 'The bombing in our area was so intense. We had nowhere to flee.'

25 JUNE 2014 ▶

Two weeks before the next big attack would start. 'Jumana's looking forward to school,' says Meysa. 'Her hand is strong, but other children ask her about it a lot. Jumana's shy. I'm remarried and am expecting another child. Jumana's looking forward to it. She wants a brother or sister.'

25 JUNE 2014 ▶

Jumana at home in al-Zaytoun. We are carefree and happy to see each other again. Little do we know that another fifty-one days of bombing will start just two weeks later.

18. JULY

TWO OLD MEN ON A BLUE BENCH

A LITTLE BOY IS SITTING MOTIONLESS on a hard blue metal bench. His small but serious face is framed by a blue shawl, and two bare feet are sticking out from beneath the shawl's white edging. His body is otherwise hidden underneath the sizeable garment.

He can only see out of one eye. His left eye is sealed completely shut and swollen a mauve shade. In the distended area below the eye, blood plasma seeps out from a small cut. A plaster has been applied diagonally from his forehead, above his left eye, over his temple and under the edge of the blue shawl. The child's delicate mouth is half open, not a sound coming out.

He is a child with the expression of an old man. His eyes are fixed forward, and his face looks as if it had turned to stone. Here is a boy, I think to myself, who has already seen more than most of us would in our entire lifetime.

Now the boy is waiting to have stitches put in the cut above his eye, which will be painful, as we have neither the resources nor the right kind of anaesthetic for everybody. This is because some people want it to be like this; they want the hospital to be short of everything and want things to hurt. They want you to lose heart and give up your dream of being free. They want you to surrender.

Those people have already started setting

up this boy for his life as an old man, sitting on a blue bench, in the eternal waiting room of his own future.

The night has given up keeping us in darkness. We try to get an overview of the situation, taking care of those with lesser injuries who have had to wait throughout the blood-stained night. I head to an overcrowded, cramped room with two examination tables and the equipment needed to clean and stitch wounds. This room always smells of blood, bodies and sweat, and it is generally filled with screams of pain from children being stitched up with insufficient anaesthetic.

Then I see him. Lying outstretched on the tattered, three-seater metal bench where the little boy was sitting a few hours earlier. The man is old, and his bare feet are sticking out from the end of the bench. His brown, ankle-length kaftan is drenched in blood around the collar and on his chest. He is holding his left hand over his chest, as if to protect himself. A bandage has been applied all the way round his head, the white material covering his eyes, but he peeks out at me through a small gap in the bandage above his right eye. An empty expression. To me, the bearded man looks dejected and exhausted. I can see that he is breathing normally, and I look across at the nurse, who nods in the direction of the stitching room.

'He's next,' he says curtly. It is his turn to be stitched up.

We can mend the small wounds, I think to myself. The deeper wounds will always be there.

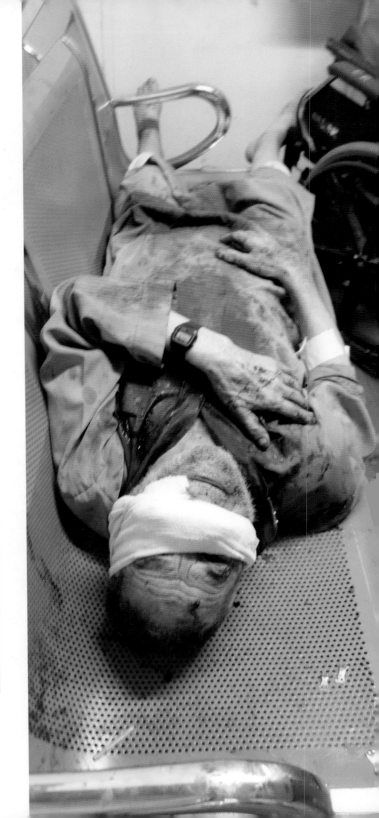

20.18

Typical life-threatening shrapnel trauma resulting from Israeli shelling. When artillery shells and bombs explode, hundreds of razor-sharp metal splinters, large and small, are dispersed at high velocity over large areas. The shrapnel can dig deep into the cranial, chest and abdominal cavities, where they can tear open blood vessels and internal organs, causing extensive internal bleeding. Even large bones in the legs and arms can be broken. This patient has been stabilised in the resuscitation room, but his life is still endangered by massive internal bleeding. This race against time will determine whether he lives or dies. If patients with shrapnel wounds survive, they need advanced post-operative care, often including many further operations and major repacking procedures for their wounds. The more patients that are saved, the greater the hospital's problems with capacity and work pressure become.

18. JULY

STRUCK BY SHRAPNEL

THE ATTACK HAS BEEN GOING ON for ten days.

Yesterday evening, the first Israeli tanks rolled into Gaza. The ground invasion had begun. It was a busy night, and many badly wounded people came to al-Shifa. The invasion started in the south of Gaza, from the border with Israel to the east, while Israeli naval vessels unleashed intense artillery fire from the sea. Fire from both sides, or actually from three sides, as the aerial attacks have not only continued, but have seen a major increase in frequency and ferocity. It appears that the Israeli forces intend to expand what they call the 'security barrier' along the border between Israel and Gaza.

The intense bombardment hit hard across the north of Gaza. Advancing Israeli tanks shelled a residential building in the north-eastern town of Beit Lahiya, near the border crossing with Israel at Erez. Three siblings were killed in their bedroom: Walaa (12) and her two brothers Mohammed (14) and Ahmed (11). They were all children of the Abu Musallam family.

Sizeable ground units stand ready at the border with Gaza. There is an uncomfortable feeling in the air. Everybody is thinking about what lies in store when the massive Israeli Merkava tanks fire their guns at overcrowded residential areas. Gaza is extremely densely populated, with 20,000 inhabitants per square kilometre in the towns, and the civilian population cannot flee or seek refuge in shelters. Most of us remember the fearful days of the ground invasion in January 2009.

It will hardly be any less bloody this time.

During a break, I see online that the Israeli government has stated that the objective of the ground invasion is limited to destroying tunnels. Dr. Abu Rish, one of the hospital managers, tells me that the Israeli ground forces have moved in from the border, across the agricultural areas in the south, towards the town of Khan Younis. At least nine Palestinians have been killed, four from the same family. The Israelis claim that they have found more than twenty tunnel exits.

'If there was no siege, there would be no tunnels. And if there was no occupation, there wouldn't be any rockets,' I say.

Now the shrapnel wounds will really start coming. The large shells from Israeli tanks and other guns shatter into thousands of sharply pointed fragments. These splinters are razor-sharp and are projected at high velocity. If the shrapnel hits people, it cuts its way through clothes, through the outer and inner layers of the skin, muscles, blood vessels and nerves, and into the body's cavities. In the cranial, chest or abdominal cavities, these fragments can cause severe and lethal internal bleeding. The heavier the fragments are, and the faster they are travelling, the worse the wounds will be. If they hit the thigh or the upper arm, bones are shattered. Treating life-threatening shrapnel wounds is difficult and time-consuming, with the lifesavers always fighting against the clock. Any internal bleeding must be found and stopped as quickly as possible.

19.20 ▶

An elderly Palestinian woman in the emergency department. She keeps looking around in confusion, as if she has no idea of what is happening.

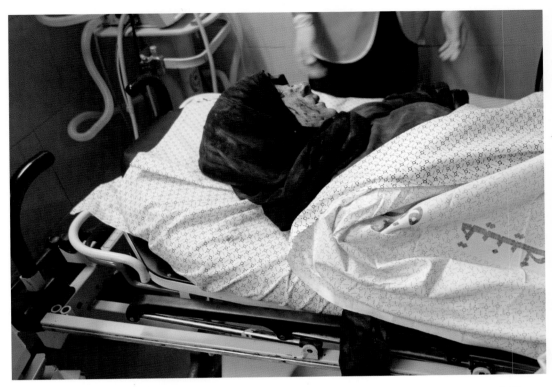

19.19 ▶

A distressed Palestinian man in the area of the emergency department reserved for the dead and the dying. He came here together with two members of his family who had been killed. I remember him shouting towards the sky. He tore the bottom of his shirt out from behind his belt to cover his face while he cried in desperation.

19.20

An injured girl comes in with lacerations to her hand and neck. They are not life-threatening, but they are frightening enough for a child. Her parents are not there, and we have no idea where they are. Every patient needs to be comforted, but there is little time, and the staff are absolutely exhausted.

The pieces of shrapnel vary in shape and size, but are all heavy, with razor-sharp edges. The larger fragments can chop off entire body parts, while the smaller ones can leave deep, life-threatening wounds.

19.27 ▶

A little boy covered with small lacerations, shrapnel wounds to his head and both eyes sealed shut. He is inconsolable, screaming unstoppably. As he cannot open his eyes, he is blinded. He tries to feel his way with his delicate hands. 'Where am I? Where's my mummy? What happened?'

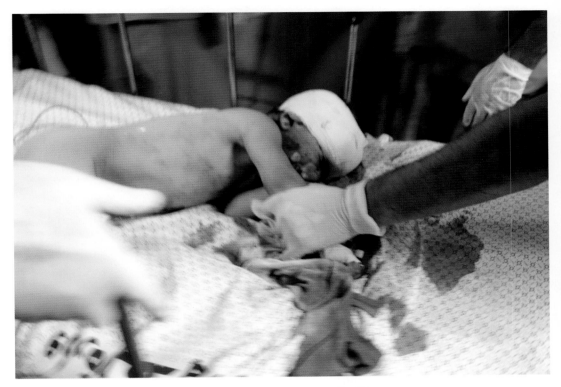

19.37 ▶

In the emergency department. He tries to find something to hold onto. I try to comfort him, but without success. His uncle fares no better. I feel desperate: we do not have the resources for anaesthesia.

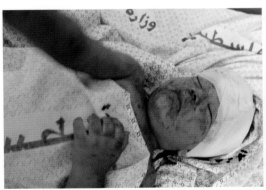

19.39 ▶

Still in the emergency department. The boy has calmed down a little, and we are about to clean his wounds. He is alive and breathing well. He will survive.

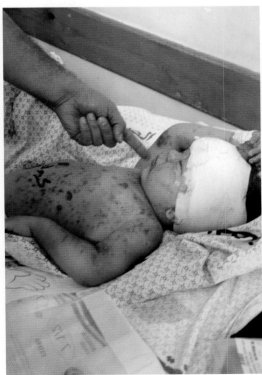

◀ 20.18

I am worn out and dripping with sweat after a
hard shift. Dr. Sobhi comes to check on us in the
emergency department. He is an excellent manager,
not only keeping an eye on the big picture but also
inspiring us all, and leading the way in the humane
treatment of all patients, respect for each other
even when the going gets tough, and maintaining a
friendly sense of humour.

▲ 22.32

We take a breather in the open space in front of the entrance
to the surgical block. There is a strong camaraderie at
al-Shifa and in Gaza, in spite of all the difficulties. Many of
the health workers at al-Shifa have been working practically
non-stop for eleven days now. I am sitting between two
colleagues with whom I have worked throughout the three
most recent attacks on Gaza: Dr. Issam Abu Ajwa and Dr.
Aiman Awadallah. The respect and admiration I have for
them is hard to describe.

PEOPLE OF GAZA:
CHRONIC HOPE

SHE LOOKS AT ME WITH A slight smile, almost teasing me. Her bright blue hijab is perfectly arranged around her girlish face.

'You don't believe it? Believe me, Dr. Mads, that's how much we have to do on our shifts: between forty and fifty births a day in the maternity ward at al-Shifa, half of which are natural births and the other half caesarean sections. When I'm on shift, I often perform ten to twenty caesarean sections a day. It's a lot, but many women in Gaza have a great number of children, and if they've had a caesarean section once, then their next children will be delivered the same way. We worked thirty-hour shifts throughout the attacks, every third day. Often it was even more, as so many other hospitals had to close due to bombing or the lack of equipment. Everybody came to us. It was terribly difficult.'

Nashwa talks about her clinical work, full of responsibilities, as if she were an experienced gynaecologist, but she is only twenty-eight years old and graduated from al-Azhar University in Gaza in 2010. In three years, she will be a fully qualified gynaecologist and obstetrician, but that will not be until 2017.

We are sitting at a hotel in Amman, the ceasefire has just come into effect and things have calmed down. Nashwa is on her way to London, while I am heading into Gaza. She has been given a scholarship to take part in a course on foetal medicine and human genetics, a speciality not currently found in Gaza. She is looking forward to it, but dreading it at the same time.

'It'll be terrible to be away from Gaza, from my family and friends, especially Jasmin. There's no place like Gaza. Even with the war and the blockade, it's a beautiful place. I come from Gaza; my family's lived there for generations. I love Gaza.'

I met Nashwa and Jasmin as fourth-year students when I was teaching them emergency medicine at al-Azhar University in 2007. They were incredibly motivated and hard-working. We next met during the attacks in 2009, when they both came to volunteer at al-Shifa, where Nashwa's father is the hospital's medical director and head of the surgical department. They stayed at the hospital, working all day and all night for three weeks. It would be the first of three Israeli attacks the two young doctors would experience in the space of just five years.

'We've got shortages of everything,' she told me when I interviewed her for the UN report I wrote in June 2014, just before the most recent hostilities broke out. 'We don't have the right kind of suture materials, we lack instruments and monitoring equipment. We don't have a canteen, a dressing room or showers. We're using the absolute minimum of resources, but we're doing our best. The blockade makes every single aspect of life very difficult. We haven't been paid our salaries for eleven months. Things like this only happen in Gaza. It's not a natural disaster, but an intentional political plan.'

'But why don't you leave? Stay in London? Emigrate?'

'I'll never leave Gaza. God has chosen me as a survivor. Now I've survived four attacks since 2006. It's a sign. I'm alive, my family's alive, our house is still standing. I've survived everything, so the message is clear. I want to give back what I've been given. I'm made to do this job and to take on this responsibility. If your country and your people need you, you have to give something back, both because I'm a Muslim and, equally, a human. Dad has been an enormous influence on me, both as a person and as a doctor. Gaza and my family have made me what I am.'

'But what about all the difficulties? The bombs, the siege, the shortages at the hospital?'

'Difficulties make us stronger, and adversity helps us to grow. We've got problems in Gaza, but we survive. Mahmoud Darwish, our national poet, said that we Palestinians suffer from a chronic illness of hope. I know what he means. And our people are like a helping hand through war and other struggles. I'm sure that we have a bright future ahead of us. It will take time, but the Palestinian people will triumph.'

'If you had to choose four things to sum up Gaza for you, Nashwa, what would those be?'

She stops to think for a brief moment.

'Hope, steadfast resistance, generosity and kindness.'

20. JULY

THE MASSACRE
OF SHUJA'IYYA

AT ELEVEN O' CLOCK IN THE MORNING on 19 July, the Israeli attack began on Shuja'iyya, a district on the eastern edge of Gaza City. The Israeli ground forces, headed by the Golani Brigade, attacked with tanks and heavy mortars, supported by F-16 fighter-bombers, initially meeting little by way of Palestinian resistance. Late in the evening, however, the Israeli forces came up against surprisingly heavy opposition from the Palestinian militia, especially the Izz ad-Din al-Qassam Brigades, which are the armed wing of Hamas. The considerably fierce fighting went on throughout the night into the morning of 20 July. Over the course of the attack, at least 140 Palestinians were killed and hundreds wounded. 13 Israeli soldiers were killed, and 56 wounded.

The power was out in Shuja'iyya, and those living there had no real escape options. Paramedics could not reach many of the injured due to the violent bombardment, while ambulances were also fired at, and ambulance workers wounded and killed. Israeli F-16 fighter-bombers dropped 100 one-tonne bombs on densely populated residential areas. Meanwhile, 11 Israeli artillery battalions deployed over 250 guns, sending at least 7000 high-explosive shells raining down on the area. According to US military sources, 4800 of these were fired in the space of just seven hours, when the attack was at its most intense.

'The only possible reason for doing that is to kill a lot of people in as short a period of time as possible,' commented one high-ranking US officer.

During the night of 19–20 July, al-Shifa received several hundred injured patients, as well as close to fifty dead or dying.

The attacks on the neighbourhood of Shuja'iyya were condemned by the UN and the EU.

Only ten days later, Israeli shells struck Shuja'iyya again, this time targeting a busy marketplace, where at least 27 were killed and over 200 injured. Al-Shifa was soon overflowing with patients again.

FACTS

FATALITIES

The Palestinian casualty figures for the period from 7 July to 28 August 2014 were the highest since 1967. The proportion of civilians killed or wounded was extremely high.

Killed

- 2220 Palestinians and 71 Israelis were killed
- 1492 are believed to be civilians
- 123 could not be identified or their status established
- 605 were identified as members of armed groups

Among the civilians killed were:

- 551 children (187 girls, 313 boys)
- 299 women

Moreover, 742 of those killed belonged to 142 Palestinian families that lost three or more family members in the same incident due to the destruction of residential buildings.

SOURCES: OCHA-oPt, 'Fragmented Lives: Humanitarian Overview 2014', March 2015; Ministry of Health, Gaza.

Large groups of wounded
patients are arriving. We wait
anxiously, everybody set,
gloves on, high readiness.

In the disaster reception area. Beneath the green material lie two children. A nurse pulls off the cover. I force myself to look. One of them, a boy seven years old in briefs and a jumper, has his rib cage and stomach covered with small cuts, his left arm dislocated with large wounds, and his head completely severed from his body. The other, a girl nine years of age, is missing half of her head and face, her right hand completely crushed. She is barefoot, wearing a plain T-shirt and knee-length tights, lying with her feet alongside her brother, reaching half-way down his body.

I feel numb and cannot stand to look. Reality is worse than our imagination. I hesitate, lift up my camera, take three pictures and turn away. The shouting in the reception area rises and falls, in lament and anger, with both prayers and battle cries. Families come running in. The shouting is rhythmical. *'Allahu Akbar!'* God is great!

Nobody can immediately identify the children, or their parents, who were also killed in the same attack. This entire Palestinian family was annihilated tonight: the two children, Umama (9) and Khalil (7), their father, Osama Khalil Ismael al-Hayya, and their mother, Hallah Saqer Hasan al-Hayya. They all lived in Shuja'iyya, in Gaza.

FACTS

THE WOUNDED

11,231 Palestinians were wounded, according to the most recent figures.

Based on early figures, among those wounded were:

- 3374 children
- 2088 women
- 410 elderly
- Up to 1000 of the wounded Palestinian children are expected to have a permanent disability
- Up to 1500 orphaned Palestinian children will need long-term support from child protection and welfare agencies

SOURCES: OCHA-oPt, 'Fragmented Lives: Humanitarian Overview 2014', March 2015; OCHA-oPt, 'Gaza: Initial Rapid Assessment', 27 August 2014; Ministry of Health, Gaza.

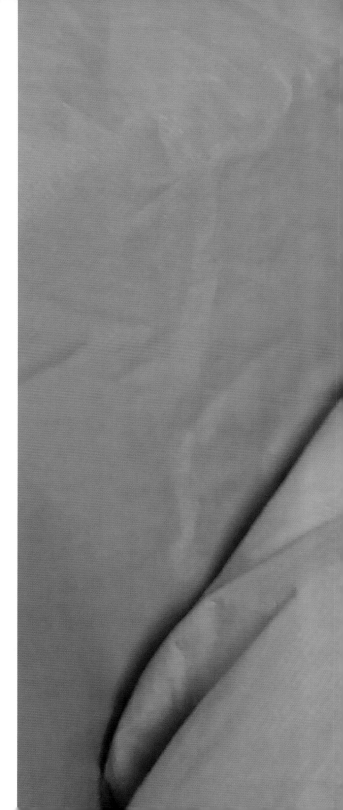

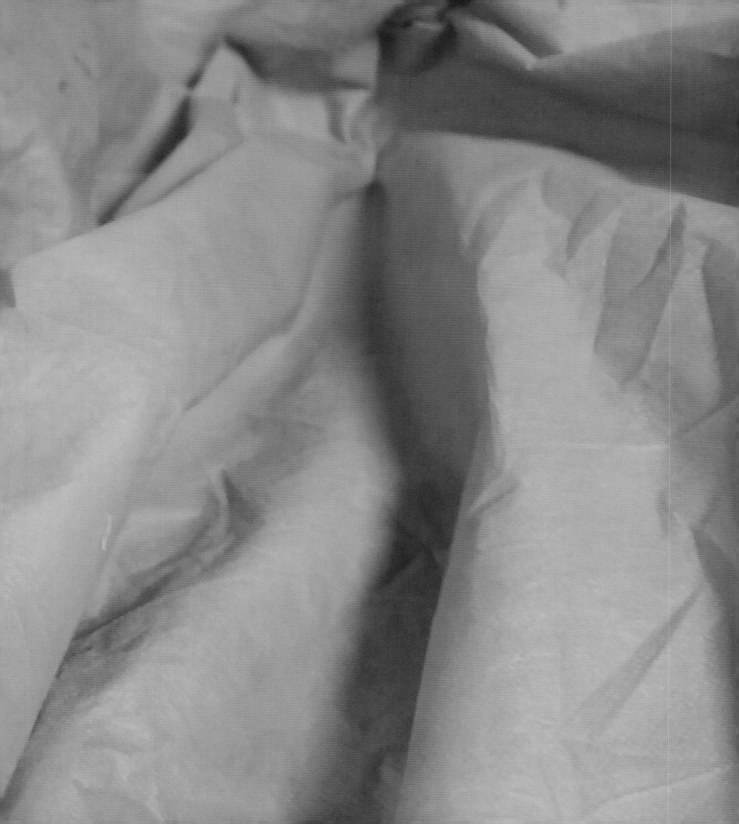

◄ **02.39**

In the disaster reception area. Dr. Yousef Abu al-Rish, Deputy
Minister of Health, makes a passionate plea next to the stretcher
where the two dead children lie. 'I have no more words,' he shouts.
A sea of Palestinian and Arab journalists fight for space around
him and the two decapitated children. Everything is documented in
photographs, video, sound and images. No details are hidden away.
The Arab world gets to see this, but hardly anything of what we
saw at al-Shifa that night got out in the Western media. The Israeli
Defence Forces told all the foreign journalists to stay at their hotel,
which they did. 'For their own safety,' as they said. The first Western
journalists arrived at around 08:30, after the massacre.

▲
02.54

Hospital workers watch the sky. More F-16s? Drones? Flares?
Is al-Shifa going to be bombed too? There is an anxious and
nervous tension, but still nobody runs off, nobody cracks.
Everybody does their job.

◀ 02.54

Large groups of families
gather outside the emergency
department. Who has been
killed? Who has been wounded?
Which houses have been
bombed? Nobody knows. We can
only guess from the sounds of
the bomb blasts. Some receive
desperate calls on their mobiles
from their families, who are
trapped. 'We need ambulances,'
they shout out into the night.
The ambulances cannot get
there. There is no safe passage,
no protection.

◀ 02.54

Outside the emergency department.
Casualties stream in. Even in the
most chaotic situations of fear and
uncertainty, the Palestinians remain
courteous. All meetings between
people, even very short ones, begin
with a firm handshake, clear physical
contact, a straight look and a
greeting: 'as-salaam alaykum', peace
be with you, or its shorter version,
'salaam'. Or alternatively 'ahlan',
welcome. This demonstration of
humanity spreads calm and dignity
in a painful fellowship born out of a
shared fate. They are saying that they
see each other: I see you, I hear you.
They share a bond that is recreated
every time they meet. Human
fellowship and respect. It builds trust

03.52 ▶

A wounded boy with his wounded
father. They can both walk and
talk, so they were assessed just
inside the door and to the left at
the entrance to the emergency
department, bandaged up
and sent back out. We do not
have enough space. Where will
they go now? Their home, their
neighbourhood, the whole area
where they live is under intense
bombardment. The young boy
looks at me gloomily. I feel as
if he is pleading with me for a
moment, saying to me: 'You're a
white foreigner; can't you get this
madness to stop? You and your
people have power. Your leaders
are supporting this. Can't you stop
it?' I feel powerlessness and guilt.

04.43 ▶

Intense concentration in the
operating theatres, all six of which
are hard at work. Many patients
are waiting. Dr. Ayman Sir is a
young vascular surgeon with wide
experience of war surgery, born
in Gaza, educated in Gaza and
staying in Gaza. 'People need us.'
Throughout the night, the system
is stretched to the extreme, with
everybody putting in maximum
effort. We concentrate on our
own tasks, as nobody has the
full picture. According to the
hospital management, around
four hundred patients came to
the hospital that day and night,
with approximately fifty dead on
arrival, or dying.

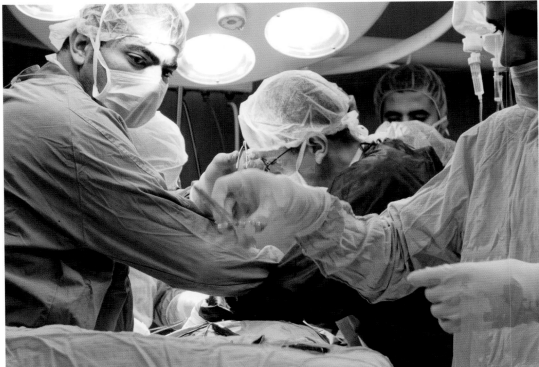

◄ 04.54

On my way from theatre to the emergency room, I look out of the west-facing window. Large groups of people are wandering restlessly along the road outside the surgical block, crying in despair, some barefoot, confused. Their faces are pale and shocked. Women trying to make sure their children stay together. The exodus from Shuja'iyya, seeking out al-Shifa as their last sanctuary. Their world is ablaze.

▲ 04.50

The hospital has a small garden area situated between its buildings. Now the garden is quickly filling up with displaced people from Shuja'iyya who have fled on foot from the merciless Israeli bombing. 'Shuja'iyya is Sabra and Shatila all over again,' says one of them. 'They're avenging the loss of thirteen Israeli soldiers in combat,' says another. 'They're going berserk now, bombing everything. Absolutely everything.'

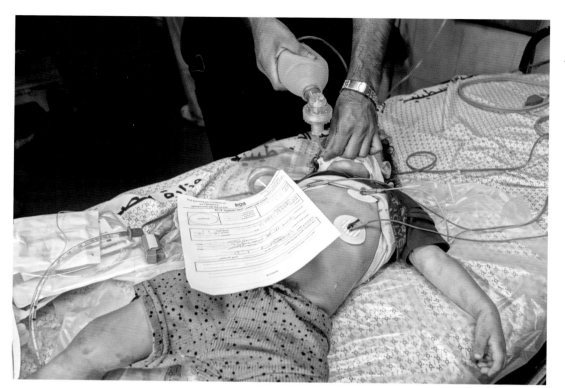

The emergency room is full of severely injured children. We intubate a little boy with head trauma. His documentation is limited. Everybody is in deep concentration, and the mood is a sombre one.

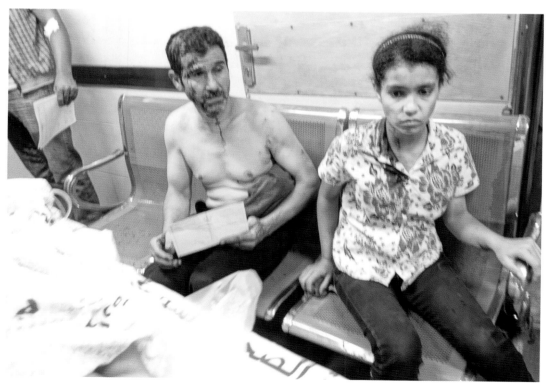

The emergency department reception area is also overcrowded. Shocked, undressed, bleeding and confused, those with lesser injuries try to understand what is happening. We do not have time to give them much information. I feel desperate: there are so many people we should be comforting. 'Stay focused,' I whisper to myself. 'Find a patient you need to help.'

04.59 ▶

Chaos. I trip, almost dropping my camera. 'Regain your balance,' I say to myself. 'Walk calmly. Speak clearly. Listen when you need to listen and speak when you need to speak. You can't take more than one patient at a time. We can do this, together we can do it. We have this under control, and if we don't have it under control, we'll get it under control.'

04.59 ▶

In the emergency room. Another child in a critical condition. Conscious. Shrapnel has made a small entry wound on the left shoulder, but has left massive damage to blood vessels and nerves in the armpit. The child's arm is threatened. This is an urgent case.

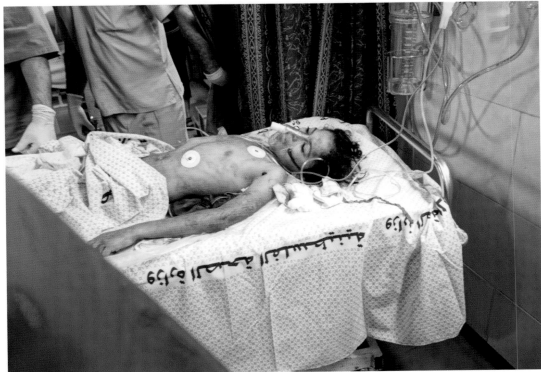

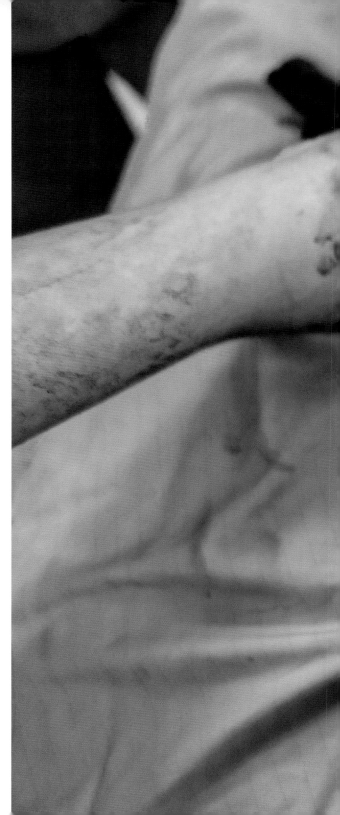

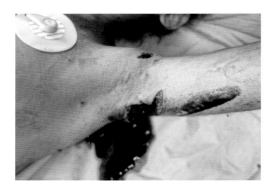

04.59 ▶

Here is a patient I need to help. A young girl with a shrapnel wound to her left shoulder. Her arm is in danger, and she needs to be operated on immediately. She is conscious and breathing on her own. We give her oxygen and intravenous fluids, and she is prioritised for immediate surgery. We have to administer a quick emergency anaesthetic. The entry wound made in her shoulder by the shrapnel is quite small, but the exit wound is like a crater. In the armpit is the artery leading to the arm, as well as a nerve plexus and important muscular attachments. If the wound is not repaired, she could lose her arm.

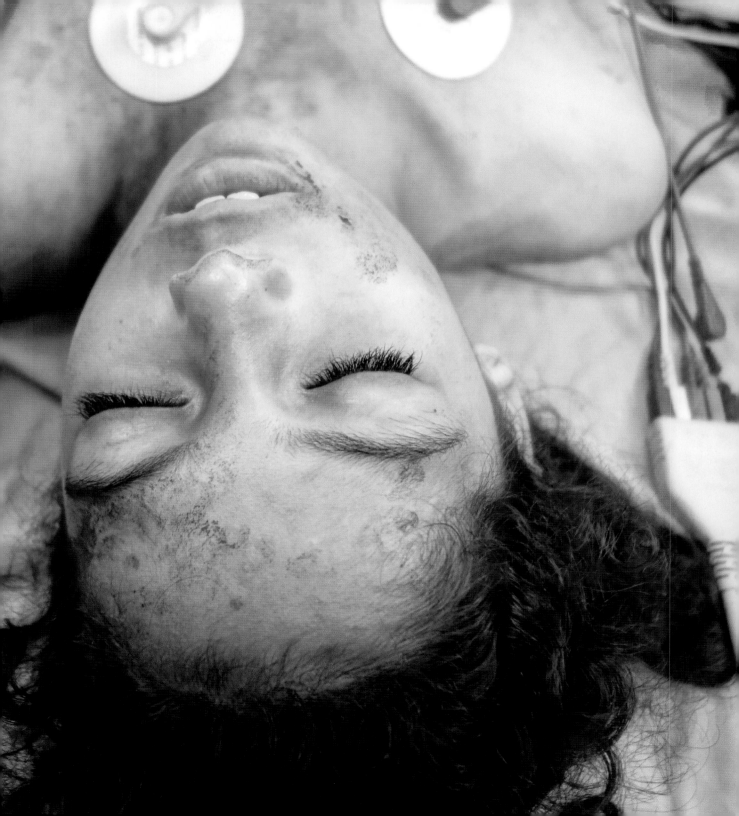

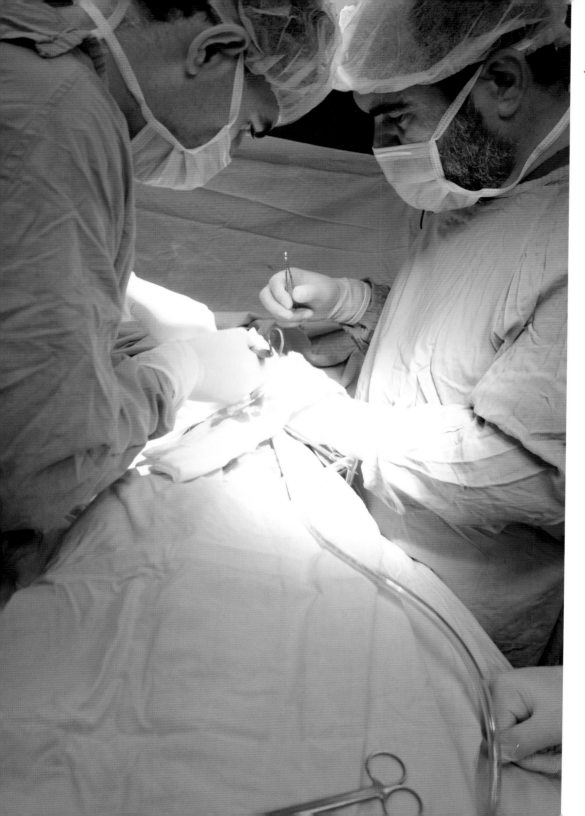

05.09

We move quickly to the first available operating theatre. She falls asleep with a small dose of ketamine. Her pain is over, for the moment. 'We'll do our best,' I whisper. The Palestinian surgeons are highly skilled, deeply and unflinchingly focused.

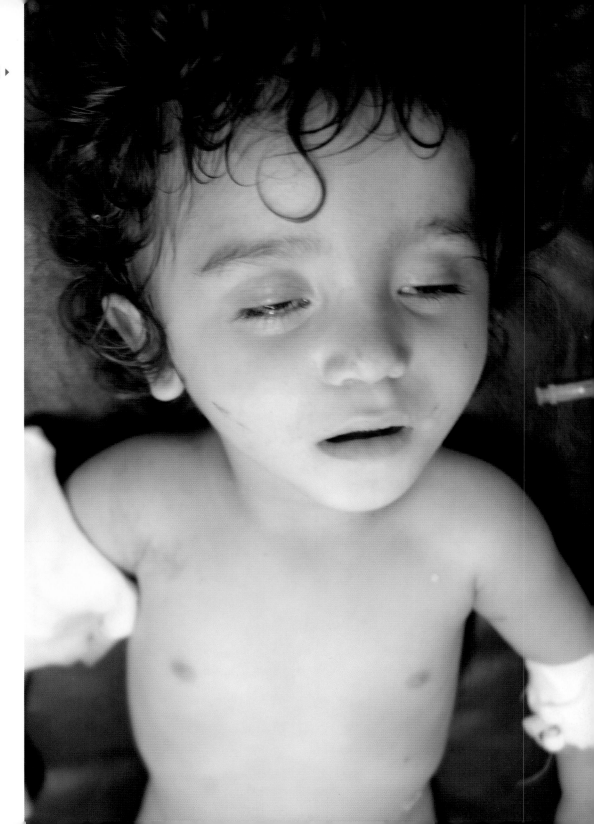

In the resuscitation room. This little girl has a deep shrapnel wound in her left thigh, almost down to the femur. The wound has to be thoroughly cleaned. She does not need a general anaesthetic, but I will not make do with local anaesthetic, so I give her the best emergency option: just the right dose of the wonder drug ketamine to induce a painless and peaceful sleep, while she continues to breathe and remains stable. I wrap her up so she will not get cold. She is not dead, but quietly sleeping. 'We'll take good care of you, little one,' I think to myself. It calms me to see how peaceful she is. I think about Maria, my youngest grandchild, playing back home in Norway, carefree in the summer sun. People are probably calling it the best summer in living memory. Here it is the worst summer in living memory. Everything is so close in the world today, and yet so far away.

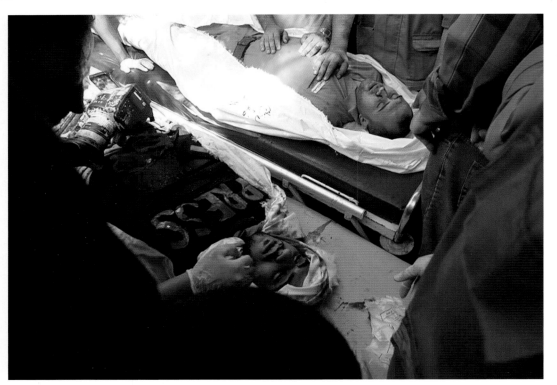

In the emergency department. Two fatalities arrive. We are aghast, many of us crying. Fouad Jaber, an ambulance paramedic, and Khaled Riyad Hamad, a journalist, were both twenty-five years old and were both killed by Israeli rockets while Fouad's ambulance was trying to evacuate casualties from Shuja'iyya, one of the first ambulances on the scene. They were in a clearly marked ambulance, and Khaled was wearing a flak jacket clearly marked 'Press'. He was trying to document the fearless work of ambulance crews to save the wounded.

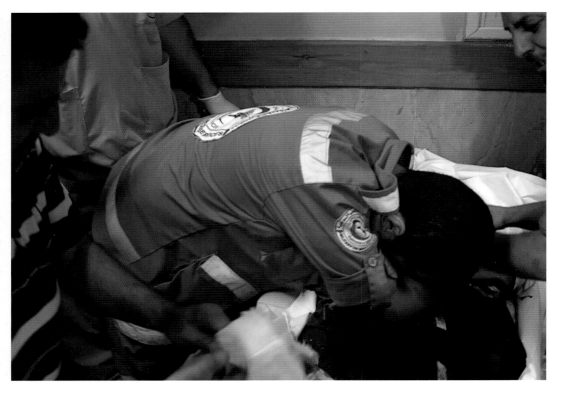

The children from this family
came to the emergency
department after they were
bombed. While their mother
searches for other members of
the family, the eldest brother and
sister have to look after the baby.
Children in Gaza take on great
responsibility at an early age.

◀ A long night in Gaza. This man, exhausted, is waiting desperately for news of his family outside the main entrance.

In the disaster reception area. At the end of the room, by the windows facing the Mediterranean, the morning sun comes flooding into the hospital. The air trembles with silence. There are no more words, no more screams; only powerlessness and certainty. That emptiness when all energy has been spent. There she sits at the end of the long room: Mother Palestine. I recognise her from so many paintings, a woman who has been carrying her burden ever since 1948, right up until today. Now she is being hunted again, bombed and subjected to attempted murder. Barefoot, with a white shawl over her hair compensating for a hijab she had to leave in the chaos of fleeing. She looks at me with an impenetrable, steady gaze. Motionless, not batting an eyelid, not shedding a single tear.

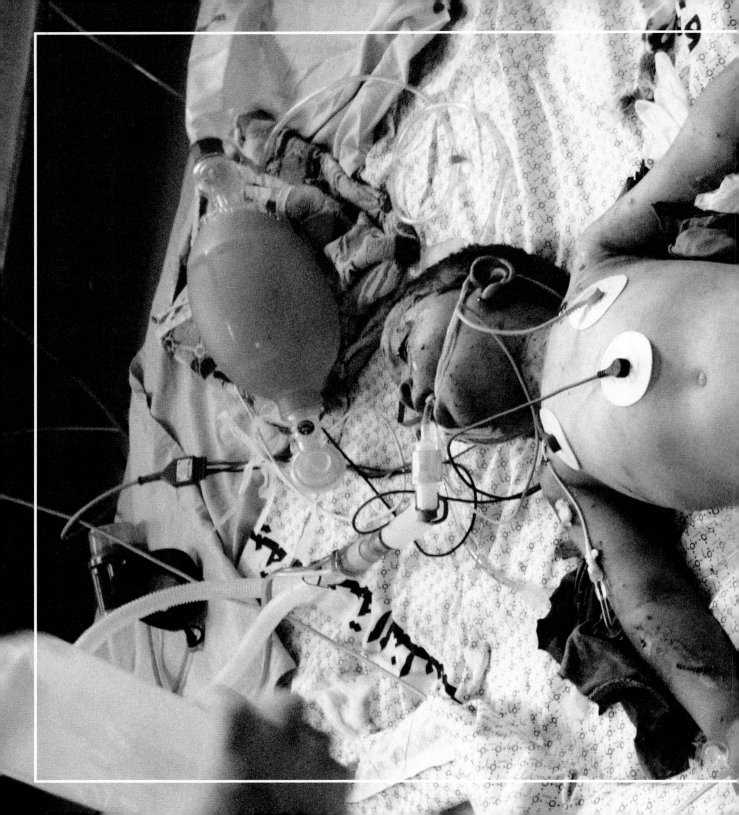

20. JULY

THE BURNT CHILDREN

THE MOOD IS TENSE. EVERYBODY IS ready to run and meet the next load of casualties.

The entrance to the emergency department soon fills with stretchers and running ambulance crews. The area begins to swarm with civilians, with and without visible injuries, policemen in blue camouflage uniforms pushing journalists and cameramen out of the way, while medical workers flock around the newly arrived patients. The air is a cacophony of shouts, screams, and sharp commands from the senior surgeon in charge of sorting the casualties. Loudest and most piercing is the unbearable sound of children shrieking.

Two young boys, one aged two or three and the other maybe seven, are both lying on a stretcher. They have visible burn injuries and a large number of small, black wounds on their faces and necks, some of them bloody, like traces of shrapnel. Dr. Atta al-Mzainy looks at me sharply.

'We've got to take them to the intensive burn care unit. Straight away,' he shouts. 'We can take one each. You take the younger one.'

'OK,' I answer, my heart pounding. Everything is collapsing around us now, I think to myself. The bombing throughout the night, the number of casualties; it all feels like a tidal wave of blood and screams. Insurmountable. I feel quite stunned as the scale of the attacks in Shuja'iyya begins to dawn on us. Over 100,000 people live in that part of town, and we have heard continuous blasts all night. The stream of casualties coming to al-Shifa has been steadily growing. A never-ending wail of sirens has announced arrival after arrival of patients torn to pieces.

I look down at the two burnt boys. Atta's clear commands and sharp gaze help. I compose myself and gently lift up the small boy, noticing that his airway is open. He is breathing. Very quickly. His screaming is loud high-pitched and hoarse, a terrible sound, and yet reassuring too. Now I know for sure that he is conscious and taking in oxygen. The sound is no less painful when I take hold of him, brushing against the areas of burnt skin.

'Shhh, shhh, *kwayyis habibi, kwayyis*.' I try to calm him down, but nothing works.

'Run, Dr. Mads, run!'

We run out of the emergency department, through the chaos at the entrance, past the heavy, blue steel door, turning left past the media camera crews' untidy nesting site, pushing against the current of people fighting their way towards the emergency department. We clear a path, pushing our way forward with sharp elbows and quick shouts, as we try to protect the two young boys.

As I run, I look down at the little boy. His hair is singed on large areas of his head. The skin is loose on his forehead and across the root of his nose. His eyelids are thick and swollen, but both his eyes are open, staring out at the world with a wild expression. He has a deep cut above his left eye, and blood is coming from his ear on the same side. Does he have shrapnel inside his skull, or is it a flesh wound? His consciousness is not impaired; quite the opposite. I notice that his arms and legs are constantly moving as I run behind my colleague, terrified of tripping and dropping the boy on the tarmac.

The Israeli drones buzz above us. Can nobody stop this nightmare?

Al-Shifa Hospital's various departments are spread across a large campus site, with a small park area in the centre surrounded by low-rise buildings one or two floors in height. The surgical block is the largest of these, towering over the landscape with its five storeys, but it is still too small for the influx of patients we are having now. We cannot do anything about the bombing. We cannot prevent these injuries. We can only help the wounded.

The trick is to change gear, to rearrange the priorities we would normally use in peacetime in order to find the right casualties to treat, stabilising them and taking them to theatre or to intensive care, in a desperate attempt to save some lives. The choice is made through cold calculations based on experience: will it be possible to save this patient? Are their wounds too serious, or do they stand a good enough chance? Is it right to use an operating theatre or an intensive care bed for this specific patient? Some patients have treatable, relatively slight injuries, while others are already dying.

Sometimes, making these assessments is straightforward, but other times, it is overwhelming. When scores of patients arrive at the same time in the emergency department, the situation needs to be managed clearly, with the prioritisation carried out quickly and resolutely by an experienced and authoritative surgeon. It is a brutal race against time, and trying to get the whole picture amidst the chaos is a struggle just as brutal.

The biggest danger is hesitation, which can quickly lead to the available operating theatres filling up with patients dying on the operating tables even after the most determined attempts to save their lives. Meanwhile, other people die who might otherwise have been saved with quick and targeted damage-control surgery.

Dr. Atta and I run as fast as we can. We need to go a couple of hundred yards down towards the back of the surgical block, then towards the outpatient department, round the corner, up some steep stairs, in through a doorway and past stacks of cardboard boxes filled with intravenous fluids.

Both boys have explosive injuries, which is the collective term used for all casualties that have occurred close to an explosion. A common factor with explosive injuries is that it is impossible to know the full extent of the patient's wounds until a thorough examination has been carried out, but in

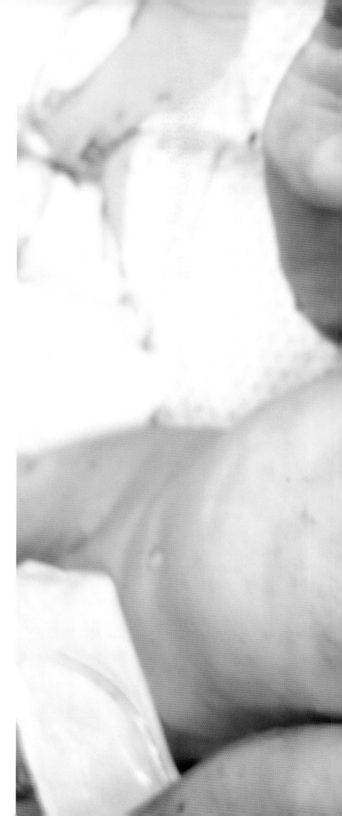

The little boy is terrified. ▶
We must anaesthetise him.

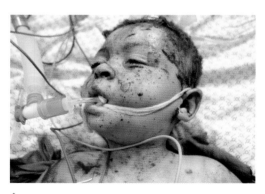

▲
The anaesthesia gives him some rest for a short while.

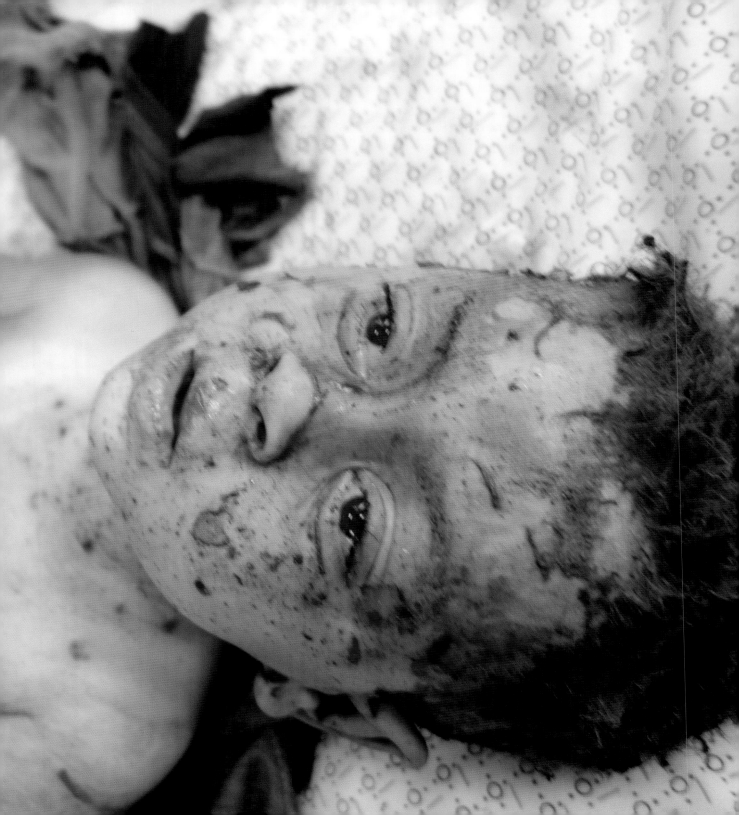

this case we have made a choice: we expect that these boys' burns are their most serious wounds. It is a risk we have to take.

'We should anaesthetise them both to secure their airways and control the pain,' I say to my colleague, in a slightly enquiring tone.

'Agreed,' he answers briefly.

We rush breathlessly into the small intensive burns unit, with its three beds. It seems the staff knew that we were coming, as two of the beds look ready. An intensive care doctor and three nurses help us. We greet each other briefly, and they point us to the beds. Greeting people is important. It is part of the basic decorum that helps us to normalise our behaviour in chaotic situations like these. We always shake hands, as long as it is practical, and establish eye contact with each other. This time we cannot shake hands because our hands are literally full, but we nod to each other. It makes us a stronger team. Respect, courtesy and human warmth are important, and they help now too, as we try to keep up our spirits.

The boy's screams are anguished and piercing. I lay him down gently on the large bed. The white quilt cover looks newly washed. At the head of the bed is a mint-green piece of cotton, of the sort we use in operating theatres. In more affluent parts of the world, we almost exclusively use packed, single-use, sterile bed sheets made from medical paper. As a result of seven years behind the Israeli blockade, there are shortages of everything at al-Shifa, even single-use sheets. They make do with their own simple solutions. A colourful bath towel lies folded on top, acting as a small pillow.

'I'll intubate him now. Can you help me?'

The nurse nods. The little boy's screams are noticeably raspier now. I am worried that his burns might also have reached his pharynx and airway. The swelling around his eyes has expanded over the course of just a few minutes. Interstitial fluid is leaking out of his cells and blood vessels; the cell walls have been damaged by the explosion and the heat, and are no longer able to retain fluid. The boy's increasingly hoarse screams are caused by his pain and fear, but they also suggest that his vocal cords have been burnt.

When we intubate a patient, we pass a sterile and relatively stiff plastic tube through their mouth or nostrils and through their oral cavity. Then, guided by sight, the tube is passed below the epiglottis, down through the upper parts of the windpipe and past the vocal cords, stopping before the windpipe divides into the two main bronchi. This procedure requires a special instrument to lift the tongue and the epiglottis, a laryngoscope, and it is so uncomfortable that it cannot be performed on a conscious patient without first administering a general anaesthetic, or by applying local anaesthesia to the mucous membranes.

Time is of the essence now. The boy's airway must be secured, so he will need a general anaesthetic.

I grab the oxygen mask and open the flow of the life-giving gas to ensure the patient's blood is sufficiently oxygenated before the hazardous procedure, giving us a little extra time in case anything goes wrong. Carefully, I put the green elastic round the back of the boy's head to keep the oxygen mask in place, leaving my hands free to prepare the medication and equipment. My hands are covered with the boy's charred, brittle hair. Just brushing against his burnt scalp sends a dust of black hair falling.

He screams even more. He does not want the mask and is panicking. We have no idea where his parents are or even what happened. We do not know what he has seen. We only know that he is badly hurt and totally distraught.

I give him a dose of ketamine pain killer deep in his thigh and ask the nurse to prepare the tube, suction and laryngoscope.

I am shaking, but I am not afraid.

Anaesthetising a conscious, wounded patient is potentially an extremely dangerous procedure even in well-trained hands, not least when the patient is a child, as the margins are smaller with children than with adults. I am an anaesthetist, so I am chiefly responsible for the patient's airway management and anaesthesia. If you take a wrong step, do not have the right medicines or know how to use the equipment needed properly, you can cause respiratory problems, falls in blood pressure, life-threatening oxygen deficiencies, brain damage or, at worst, death.

Nevertheless, the most critical factor in the situation is teamwork and communication, which is why we use a special procedure to secure a patient's airway in emergencies: rapid sequence intubation (RSI), which we train for extensively. The team's duties should be clearly divided, the equipment should be checked and laid out, the medications prepared and checked, doses worked out, and we should have an emergency back-up plan in case everything falls through, a bit like a pilot's checklists before take-off and landing in an aeroplane or helicopter. In my normal workplace in Tromsø, we regularly train for this procedure, both with the air ambulance and in the emergency medicine department. It ensures the quality of our work. Even though we speak the same language, have enough supplies and new equipment, are not being shot at or bombed, and never have the same influx of patients as here in Gaza, we still experience pressure, stress and fear of failure in many emergency situations.

Now this badly wounded and hurt little boy is to be anaesthetised, and I am working with experts I do not know. We work in different languages, use different names for instruments, procedures and drugs, and we have very different cultures, but we share something important that brings us closer together than all other factors. We are in this together. We have the same aim: survival. There is no reason to kill or maim children. They must be protected. This shared conviction of our common goal and standards creates an atmosphere of fundamental respect. Respect leads to trust, and trust generates calm and mutual support.

We can manage this, I think to myself, as I lay out the syringes with the medications needed. I prepare the syringes myself every morning and keep them in the breast pocket of my green smock, refilling them as necessary. The drugs have exotic names: ketamine, succinylcholine, atropine, midazolam, atracurium, or pancuronium and adrenaline. To most people, these may be as unfamiliar as the Latin names of plants, but they are very familiar to those of us working in anaesthesiology. It is like sweet music when somebody says the syringes are ready and sterile, each containing a given drug at the right concentration and clearly marked.

I cut up some pieces of plaster to act as labels, writing the names of the drugs and their concentrations on the syringes with a waterproof felt-tip pen. The pen is one of the things I have brought from Norway as part of the small emergency pack I take with me when I go to work in a warzone. I write simply 'K', 'S' and 'M' on the flat, circular top of the plungers on the three most important syringes, so I can quickly fish out the right one. A simple, safe and useful method that saves time. In emergency medicine, time is always a critical factor, so the more you have ready in advance, the more quickly you can act. The better a team is trained, the faster their treatment goals can be reached. The more accurately pieces of equipment and medicine are prepared, the safer our work becomes.

The dose of ketamine in the patient's thigh works well, and the boy calms down, his breathing becoming steadier, but still fast. We have managed the effective insertion of an intravenous cannula and have checked our equipment. The laryngoscope – the instrument used to lift the tongue and epiglottis out of the way – has a tiny light at the end to illuminate the throat and the glottal slit. Is the instrument working? Are the batteries and the light bulb OK? Is it lighting up? Is the plastic tube the right diameter and length? Is the suction attached and switched on? Is the bag – the plastic balloon we use to blow air through the catheter when it is in place – ready?

There is so much to look out for. Nothing must fail. 'The devil is in the details' is our watchword now. When I administer the drugs, the boy quickly loses consciousness. If we were not ready to take over his vital functions, he would die, or, more accurately, we would have killed him.

We manage it fine and with confidence.

I call out the doses, the nurse repeats them and passes the syringes without hesitation. The boy becomes totally limp, and his breathing stops. I kneel by his head, ready to intubate him. The visibility is poor. His mucosae are swollen, with blood and mucus in his throat. I try to guide in the tube, but it is hard to see, and it slips down his oesophagus. Out it comes. Suction to get rid of the mucus and blood. Another attempt. Success. I blow directly into the tube, holding it tightly between my thumb and forefinger, and I see both sides of the boy's little rib cage rise. We listen carefully and intently through the stethoscope: the tube is in the right position. Air is entering both his lungs. The numbers on the monitors are good: a good blood oxygen saturation level, good blood pressure, no tears.

Now he is sleeping deeply, without a care in the world. For a brief while.

His big brother is asleep too. The same procedure has been carried out at the neighbouring bed, and we finish at the same moment. Silence descends on the room. We can hear the sound of the drones outside, or the 'zennanis' as the Palestinians call the unmanned Israeli aircraft, the 'hummers', after the annoying sound of their engines. The blasts of the Israeli bombs continue, like not-too-distant thunder.

We cut open the boy's trousers. His genitals are also burnt. He has large blisters on the inside of his thighs, on his crotch and scrotum. We insert a urinary catheter while we still can. Burns require thorough monitoring of the body's fluid balance and large amounts of intravenous fluids for the first few days. Urine output is measured carefully on an hour-by-hour basis in order to adjust the supply of liquids. The team here know what they are doing. There is a high level of professional expertise at al-Shifa, but the lack of equipment, medicine and disposable items is wide-ranging, having a detrimental effect on the treatment. The number of casualties coming to al-Shifa Hospital every single day, week after week, is far more than well-equipped emergency units in hospitals in wealthier parts of the world would be able to take. So far, the attacks have lasted twelve days and show no signs of stopping.

Before we leave the intensive burns unit, we thank our colleagues for their co-operation. It was good to accomplish this together. Firm handshakes. A hint of a smile.

'They might be all right,' says the intensive care doctor. 'Their burns might be less extensive than we first thought, and it looks like their other wounds are superficial. Let's hope they make it!'

'Inshallah!' I answer.

'Inshallah!' he replies, as is the custom here.

The thick, grating stench of the children's burnt hair and skin is still there in my nose and in my green scrubs as we hurry back to the emergency department.

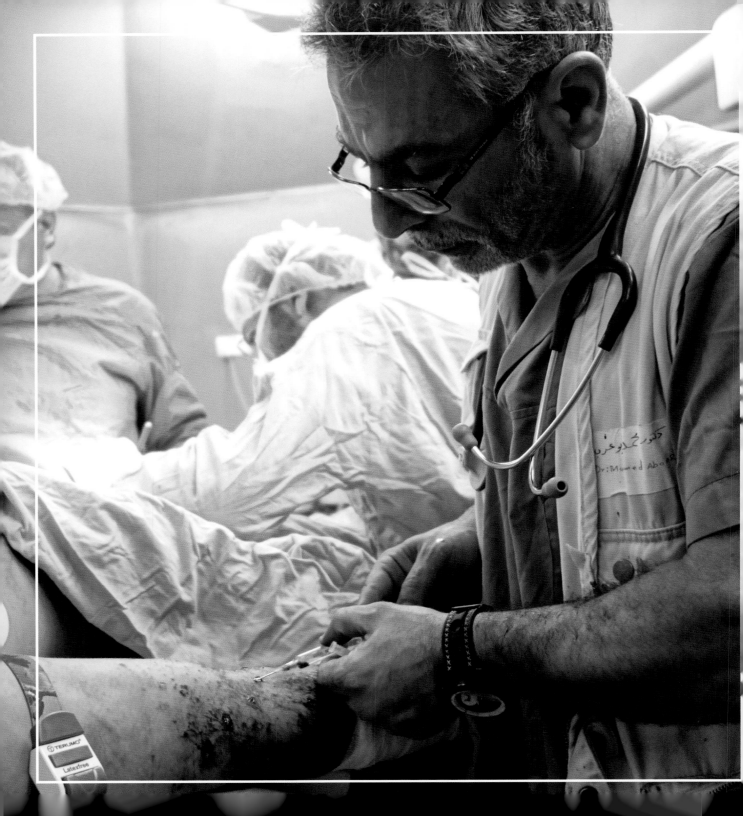

PEOPLE OF GAZA:
'I LOVE YOU'

'I'M IN!'

The text message arrived on my mobile phone with a beep. Mohammad had also managed to get into Gaza now. When we last saw each other in Cairo, everything was uncertain. Dr. Mohammad and the team from PalMed, the organisation of Palestinian doctors working in Europe, were going to try getting in again through Sinai and the border crossing at Rafah, in the south of Gaza. Now we had both succeeded, and Mohammad was on his way north, towards al-Shifa.

Mohammad is a Palestinian with Norwegian citizenship and a complex background, having spent a long time travelling as a refugee before ending up as an anaesthetist at Aker University Hospital in Oslo. Born as a Palestinian refugee in west Beirut, he received his primary education at a UN school in Shatila, the Palestinian refugee camp. Then he went away to study medicine in Ukraine, then part of the Soviet Union. From there, he travelled to Libya to work as a doctor, then to Poland and, as a refugee, onwards to Denmark, where he received authorisation and worked as a doctor for ten years, before eventually arriving in Norway in 1998. He worked at Ullevål Hospital first, and then later as a senior anaesthetist at Aker Hospital. He has always been active in the Palestinian cause.

Now he had come back to Gaza to assist his people. Holding the fort back home in Oslo was his wife, Hanaa, together with their five children aged twelve to twenty-five.

'There you are, *habibi*! What was it like getting back in?'

Standing outside the emergency department, we give each other a hug and kiss cheeks, jumping with joy to see each other again. He speaks a wonderful Danish-Norwegian-Palestinian composite language, splendidly colourful and with as many diverse roots as Mohammad himself.

'You know, we told them that President Sisi can just get stuffed! Now our story's all over the Arab media. People are so angry, you wouldn't believe it. Not letting doctors in here to help is a total disgrace. It's worse than last time!'

'Last time' was back in 2009, when Mohammad was one of the four members of the experienced crisis team that had come from Norway to take the places of Erik Fosse and me at al-Shifa. He knows what lies in store: lots of blood, horrific situations, non-stop work, traumatic experiences, limited equipment but, most of all, a strong sense of solidarity with his own people.

Dr. Mohammad is a natural authority figure, and he gives all of himself and his unstoppable work capacity day and night. He discusses our work and organisational matters, often delivering short, animated lectures while we work. He offers encouragement where it is needed, gives generous praise when somebody deserves it, and never tries to ingratiate himself with others. He is critical of professional sloppiness and is driven mad by any signs of complacency. He is always optimistic, but perhaps not so much right now.

Now it is night, and we have been here for a week.

'I don't know if I can take any more, Mads. I'm completely exhausted. Can we sit down somewhere quiet? I need to talk with you.'

Mohammad's face is drawn, unshaven and tearful. We sit down alone on a step. I fetch some sweet, warm tea in two plastic cups. We light a cigarette, and Mohammad leans against the railing, breathing in deeply.

'I have never, ever seen so many fatalities or such terrible wounds. I have never felt that they're trying to destroy us as much as now. And it just keeps on going. It's unbearable.'

I put my hand on his knee. We sit there for a long time in silence. Two ambulances with flashing red lights are outside the emergency department. Darkness shrouds the hospital. We have been going for eight days non-stop now. We are so tired.

We talk quietly and slowly about our anguish, and about how helpless we sometimes feel. How much it hurts to be there amidst so much pain and loss. About how angry we both are, as all of this could be avoided. Everybody could have been spared.

It helps to blow off steam, to listen to each other. Only a few words, but it helps.

Then we have finished our tea and are ready again.

'I love you,' I say.

'I love you, too,' Mohammad answers.

The usual farewell at al-Shifa these days every time people go their separate ways, as nobody ever knows whether we will get to meet each other again.

22. JULY
HOW DO THEY COPE?

◀ The hospital is besieged by TV vans, with
journalists reporting twenty-four hours a day.

I CANNOT UNDERSTAND HOW THEY COPE. The
Israeli attacks have now been going on for
two weeks. What are they made of, these
people? What keeps them going?

'Would you like some more Arabic coffee,
Dr. Mads?' Salah al-Haw asks me kindly.

The time is past midnight. It is relatively
quiet, apart from the chronic, unnerving
sound of the drones. We are sitting outside
the open back door of an immense Chevy Van
parked together with numerous other similar
vehicles in the car park in front of the hospital.

'When did you last get to sleep in your own
bed?' I ask him as he passes me some sweet,
steaming hot Arabic coffee in a plastic cup.

'No, I can't remember. Some time before
the war started, perhaps?'

'Two weeks non-stop?'

'Yes, that's what it's like. We work night and
day, after all. It's dangerous to move about too
much, so we sleep in the van or at the office.'

Salah is a cameraman and broadcast
technician. He works for the small Palestinian
media company MediaTown.ps, which
produces news footage and documentaries.
The company's manager, Ashraf Mashharawi,
works with his team of six employees twenty-
four hours a day to document every aspect of
the Israeli attacks. When they are not actively
filming, they stay in their van, from which
they edit and broadcast their footage, sleeping
for the few hours they can on a mattress in
the back or sitting in their seats. I have known

00.20 ▶

Taking a cup of Arabic coffee together with the cameramen from MediaTown.ps, Ashraf Mashharawi's documentary film company. Like the other Palestinian and Arab media crews, they stay at their posts outside al-Shifa day and night, when they are not filming at the front line where the bombs fall.

them since 2009, when Ashraf's eleven-year-old brother, Mahmoud, and their sixteen-year-old cousin, Ahmed, were hit by a missile from an Israeli drone while they were playing on the roof of the family home in Gaza City.

Ahmed was torn to pieces, while Ashraf's little brother was dying when he arrived at al-Shifa. I led the unsuccessful attempts to resuscitate him, but Mahmoud would never grow any older than eleven. Telling Ashraf that his brother had died was the first time I met him. It was the start of a close friendship. Ashraf made a major contribution to the documentary *Hva drepte lillebror?* (What killed my little brother?) produced by the Norwegian state broadcaster NRK and shown as part of the *Brennpunkt* strand in February 2009. This programme went behind the news about the war in Gaza to investigate the killing of the two boys, while also demonstrating the effect of Norwegian arms exports to Israel via the United States.

The young men in Ashraf's production company, the *shabab*, are good friends of mine. I meet with them every time I am in Gaza. They live dangerously, all risking their lives to document the real life of Palestinians. They get themselves close to where the bombs are

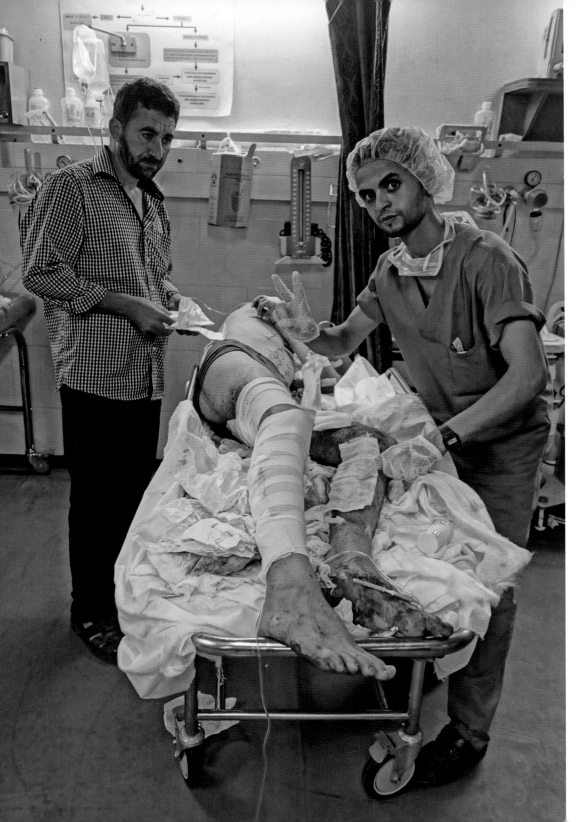

A casualty arrives in the emergency department, having been transferred from a smaller hospital. A few keywords regarding his diagnosis and treatment are written in felt-tip pen on his stomach and chest. The health workers see themselves as part of the popular resistance. The 'V for victory' sign is seen frequently.

falling, filming scenes that are soon seen in the news media around the world. All the lads have been injured, but none has been killed, so far. They are here year after year and see everything, including their own families being killed or wounded. The first journalist to be killed was from Gaza. He came to al-Shifa two days earlier, after the bombing of Shuja'iyya.

News broadcasts from al-Shifa are important. Journalists and camera crews can get breaking news at the hospital, and live pictures of the casualties and of those killed. Frequent press conferences are held by the hospital management and by the Ministry of Health on an improvised platform outside the main entrance, and it is easy to find eyewitnesses and relatives who can share their dramatic stories. Al-Shifa is also considered a relatively safe place to avoid the Israeli bombs. Although it is safer, hospitals and health centres have already been bombed, and many health workers have been killed or wounded.

The parked vans are marked with the words 'TV' or 'PRESS' spelt out in large letters with black duct tape or messily painted. Media crews use their vans for everything: as equipment stores, power sources with enormous generators, or live broadcasting units with roof-mounted satellite dishes, as well as using them for transport and as accommodation for Palestinian cameramen and journalists. They work day and night, following the rhythm of the Israeli attacks.

How do they cope?

I have been working with the Palestinians for thirty-three years, and I think I am beginning to understand how they do it.

My first encounter with the Palestinian people was in 1981, when I went to work in west Beirut for the Palestine Committee of Norway. We were the first ever 'crisis team' to travel there from Norway. Israeli aircraft had bombed the Fakhani district in the Lebanese capital, where the Palestine Liberation Organisation (PLO), the leading political force in the Palestinian resistance movement at that time, had its headquarters, as well as the bunker of its leader, Yasser Arafat. The aim of the Israeli attacks, then as now, was to kill, and to destroy organised Palestinian resistance to the occupation. Ariel Sharon – who was then the Israeli Defence Minister – and the Prime Minister Menachem Begin probably thought that, by liquidating the top leaders of the Palestinian resistance movement, they could lay the groundwork for the total Israeli takeover of the West Bank and Gaza, expelling the Palestinians to Jordan.

Yasser Arafat's brother, Dr. Fathi Arafat, led the Palestinian Red Crescent, which was, in practice, the Palestinian health ministry. He made a powerful appeal for medical aid for the bombing victims in Beirut. I was asked to organise a team and, together with the thoracic surgeon Dag Sørlie and the theatre nurse Kari Wendt, left in great haste from Tromsø Regional Hospital – as it was then called – heading for Lebanon. It was there

Shadi cleans one of the six operating theatres at al-Shifa after a surgical amputation procedure. Cleaning is vital for the management of a hospital in the midst of the catastrophes of war. The operating theatres look like blood baths and must be cleaned as quickly as possible, tidied up and prepared for the next patient. Shadi does his job efficiently and always with a ready smile. Laughter is the best medicine. The Palestinians achieve just the right balance of pitch-black humour, which helps to see them through, and deep seriousness.

we met the Arafat brothers. The refugee camps in Beirut were where I first met ordinary Palestinians, as well as the political leadership. The situation was mostly over when we arrived in Beirut, so our mission was more peaceful than expected. We ended up working at a nice little hospital in al-Buss refugee camp, in the south of Lebanon. The following year, in the summer of 1982, Israel carried out a large-scale invasion of Lebanon, laying siege to west Beirut and extensively bombing the city, with its population of over a million. This time, the Palestine Committee sent a number of surgical crisis teams, co-ordinated by the doctors Erik Fosse, in Oslo, and Ebba Wergeland, in Beirut. It was an important experience and a momentous encounter with the merciless destruction wrought by the Israeli war machine, but also an encounter with the endurance, dignity and determination of ordinary Palestinians.

Then, as now, we worked shoulder to shoulder with local health workers – then they were Palestinian and Lebanese – and volunteers to save war-wounded patients. It was a steep learning curve, as battlefield

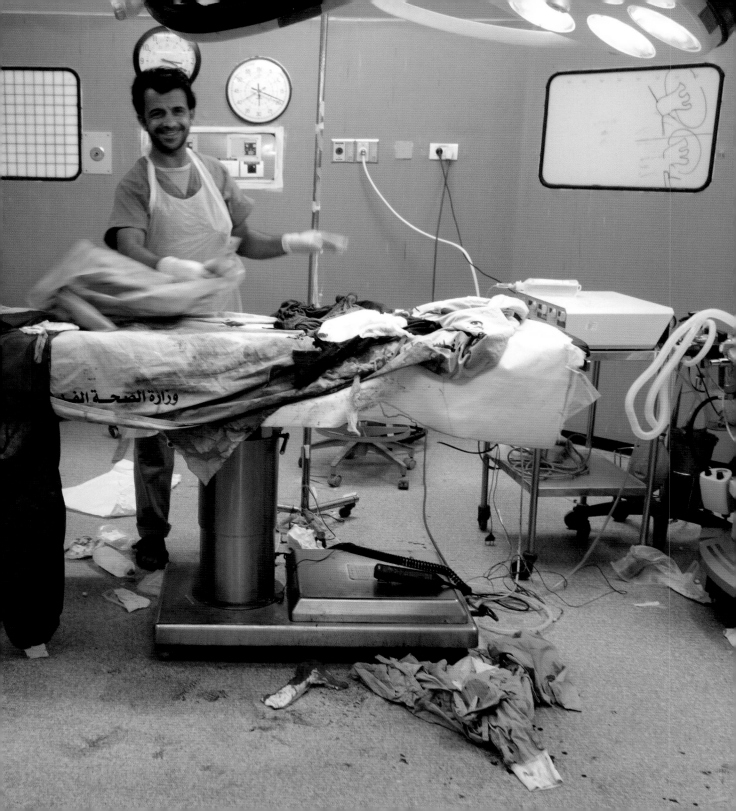

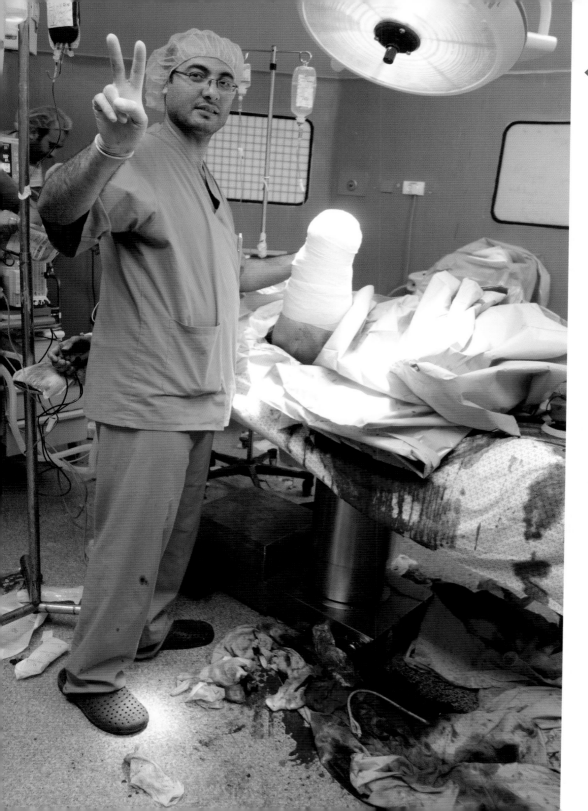

◀ 02.11

Dr. Aiman, an orthopaedic surgeon, completes yet another amputation. 'We'll never give up. We must be strong and show that the wounded are being helped.'

surgery had not exactly been part of the core curriculum when I studied medicine in at the University of Oslo. Several things were left seared into my young soul: the Palestinians' conviction about the deeply just nature of their struggle to regain their own country, their extreme perseverance, and last but not least a combination of humanity, warmth, hospitality and care for others that I had never encountered before.

There has been a clear thread running from the experiences in west Beirut in 1982 to Gaza in 2014: the merciless oppression of the Palestinian people is unjust and is contrary to international law and universal human rights. There is no military solution to the occupation of Palestine and the exile of the 5 million Palestinians who, according to the UN's official records, are still living as refugees in Gaza, the West Bank, Lebanon, Syria, Jordan and Israel.

Salah shakes me out of my thoughts.

'We just want to live as free people, like you and your family in Norway, Dr. Mads. Nobody wants to live like animals, trapped and controlled by others. We don't want to be occupied.'

An Israeli flare floats slowly through the night sky to the east, falling towards the ground in a characteristic spiral motion, lighting up roads and houses on its way. More attacks are coming. More blood will be shed. Soon the sirens will be shrieking again as the hospitals fill with many more patients wounded, dying and deceased.

This time, it is not the PLO or Arafat they are trying to wipe out. Now Hamas is the pretext for the attacks, but the reality is the same as in 1982. It is the wider, organised Palestinian resistance to the Israeli occupation that is being punished. It is not a case of 'Hamas versus Israel's right to exist', or 'terrorism versus democracy', as Netanyahu, Lieberman and Obama claim. The state of Israel intends to crush the Palestinian people's will to resist so that they can then be driven out. This is why the civilian population is being targeted. This is why half of the casualties are women and children, why schools, hospitals, ambulances, places of worship and ordinary homes are being bombed to pieces. It is collective punishment, in clear contravention of international law and the founding Charter of the United Nations, not that this matters to the Israeli war machine. Meanwhile, the international community has chosen to forget that the political party Hamas was elected with a clear majority in the democratic election carried out by the Palestinians in Gaza and the West Bank on 25 January 2006, in accordance with the wishes of the West: the first such elections in any Arab nation. The winner was the Change and Reform party, led by Ismail Haniyeh, representing Hamas. They won 74 of the 132 seats in the Palestinian Legislative Council, enough to secure them an overall majority. Fatah lost, with its 45 seats. Immediately after the election, sanctions began against the Palestinian people, who had shown the

Back on the steps. The long day ends where it ▶
began: a moment of calm together with good
friends outside the hospital.

impertinence of using their democratic right
to vote for the party they thought was best,
just as we do in our own elections. For the
Palestinians, however, the election resulted in
a blockade, economic sanctions and repeatedly
brutal military attacks by Israel.

I draw a deep breath, feeling a gnawing
anxiety in my stomach. How long can this go
on before the hospital and its organisation fall
apart? When will it all come undone? How
long can Israel keep up its attacks before the
world puts a stop to them? After all, sanctions
have just been imposed by the West against
Russia due to the situation in Ukraine, while
Israel is bombing the civilian population of
Gaza. Why are there no sanctions against
Israel? Are Palestinian lives worth less? Are
the geopolitical interests of the West, and
especially the United States, served by having
Israel act as an aggressive military power at
the expense of the Palestinians?

Nobody can say that they do not know
about it. The Palestinian Ministry of Health
and the UN organisations in Gaza issue
precise and documented figures every
single day. Journalists are reporting on the
war live. Camera crews follow us around
the emergency department, the operating
theatres, the wards and the mortuary. The
international media are here. What is it about
Israel that makes the country immune to
international sanctions from the West?

The nine-year-old Samar is kind and considerate to all her five brothers and sisters. Hajar, aged four, loves her big sister.

PEOPLE OF GAZA:
SAMAR

SEPTEMBER 2014 ON THE RAINY STREETS of Brussels. I have been testifying as a witness at the extraordinary session of the Russell Tribunal on the attacks in Gaza and am now deep in my own thoughts. The taxi driver looks at me in the rear-view mirror. He shakes his head as we turn right up a slight hill, passing by a group of young Arab men aged seventeen or eighteen.

'Don't walk about here. Call a taxi when you're heading back to your hotel. This is a dangerous neighbourhood. *C'est très dangereux!'*

The grey blocks of flats on the outskirts of Brussels are closely packed, separated from each other only by side roads with a few green lawns and trees. The area looks tired, and fog creeps between the tower blocks.

What will she look like now? How is she doing? What were her thoughts about this most recent attack on Gaza? Will she still remember me?

Samar was only four years old during Operation Cast Lead in January 2009, when the atrocity happened. Now she is almost ten and has been living here in Brussels with her family for five years. We have not seen each other since I kissed her goodbye in the paediatric surgical ward, where she was lying after having come to al-Shifa on 7 January 2009, seriously wounded. Both her sisters were shot and killed in front of her own eyes.

A SPLIT SECOND

I will always remember that moment back

then: the little girl looking at me with her big, brown eyes, as I came running into the ward to say farewell and give her a soft toy stuffed with confectionery. I had decided that the last of the presents from the duty-free shop at Oslo Gardermoen Airport would go to Samar, and she had to get it straight away.

The ambulance convoy was ready to depart. The vehicles were full of seriously wounded patients we would accompany to the southern border crossing at Rafah. They would be evacuated via Egypt to other countries with better resources for their treatment than there were in bombed-out Gaza. In the convoy, the mood was tense and impatient.

'I've just got to run up to the children's ward and say goodbye to Samar,' I told the ambulance drivers.

'*Yalla*, doctor, *yalla*!' they answered. 'We cannot wait, soon we start.'

I came into the ward, breathless, went over to her bed, stroked her unruly curls and looked straight into her inquisitive eyes.

'*Ma salaam*, Samar. Goodbye.'

I lifted up her left arm and put the toy tiger, with a plastic window in its stomach, filled with sweets, in the crook of her arm.

'*Afwan!* You're welcome,' I said quietly, bending forward. I lifted her head up a little towards me. I placed my right hand gently on her head and held her steady. I kissed her on the forehead, between her closed eyes.

Time stood still, just for a second. For one eternal, peaceful moment, there were only the two of us in the world.

I heard the characteristic click of a camera shutter and looked up to see a photographer on the other side of the bed.

'*Ma salaam*, farewell, Samar,' I whispered. 'You'll be all right.'

She looked me straight in the eye without saying a word. I turned around and went, leaving her there. I ran to the convoy.

The picture the photographer took of that moment and of the farewell kiss would follow us both over the next few years.

Brussels. A man in his forties comes walking slightly uncertainly across the grass. A pair of sunglasses, looking a little out of place, lie across his forehead. He lifts his hand hesitantly to greet me. Might it be Khaled, Samar's father? I have never met the man, but I recognise him. He was featured in the report a BBC journalist made about the 'incident', if that is what it can be called. Can the murder of defenceless children really be called an 'incident'?

Samar arrived at al-Shifa that sombre day on 7 January 2009, midway through the Israeli attack known as Operation Cast Lead. The little four-year-old was sent to the operating theatre in great haste. She lay on her back on the stretcher, stripped to her jeans and half-covered by a small quilt. Her uncertain eyes were searching in vain for familiar faces. She had come in the ambulance alone from her family's house somewhere in the north of Gaza. The Israeli bombing was so intense that the ambulances were only carrying the

Samar arrived at al-Shifa alone, four years old and badly wounded. A large crater in her back left her spinal column exposed. She was not crying and could not move her legs. I thought it was a shrapnel wound, but she had been shot. Her two sisters had been killed in the same attack.

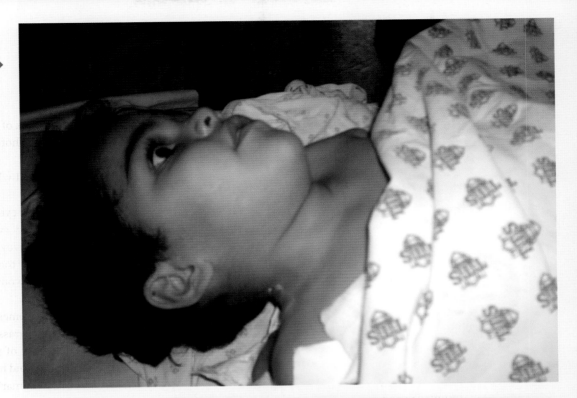

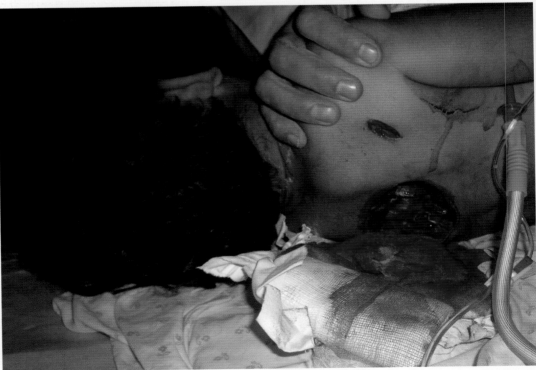

wounded and not their family members, as there was such a great danger of attacks on ambulances too. It was not clear what had happened, but no doubt her family's house had been shelled that morning. Her mother had supposedly been injured too.

Samar had wounds to her chest, with internal bleeding. In the resuscitation room, a drainage tube had been inserted into her right thoracic cavity. Her main injury was on her back, a large, gaping, open wound at the level of her shoulder blades, cutting right through to her vertebral column. Skin and tissue had been torn away, and we could see parts of the spinal column, including the bone itself. She was without feeling from the waist down and could not move her legs. Everything suggested that the spinal cord itself was damaged. She needed urgent neurosurgery to alleviate the problem.

I first saw her by the lift to the operating theatre, where I was given a short report on her condition. With the nurse accompanying her, we turned her carefully onto her side in order to inspect her wound and the bleeding. I shuddered. Was this possible? A four-year-old girl with a complete spinal cord injury caused by an act of war?

Samar was wide awake and was not crying. She looked at me intensely, studying me for a moment, before fixing her gaze somewhere on the ceiling, as if she were looking for something far away. Without doubt her mother. She was in safe hands there at al-Shifa, but she was missing her family, most of all her mother and father. I tried to take in how vulnerable she was, alone without her parents. Samar's nurses wheeled her stretcher into the rickety lift and accompanied her to the operating theatre.

At around midnight that same evening, I went up the ice-cold stairway to the third floor to do my nightly rounds of the children in the paediatric ward. Dr. Hamid Abu Ubaid, the neurosurgeon who had operated on Samar, was able to confirm our shared pessimism: the spinal cord injury was total and irreparable. She had suffered a complete cross-sectional lesion and would remain paralysed below her chest for the rest of her life.

'We Palestinians have no human rights,' Dr. Hamid answered when I asked him in desperation how these brutal attacks on civilians could still be going on.

Samar lay in the middle one of three large beds in Room 545. She had a thick plastic tube through her nose and intravenous cannulae in both arms. She was crying softly.

'Mama, mama, mama, mama.'

She was crying and calling in whispers for her mother. Endlessly. The women sitting with the two other wounded children in the neighbouring beds did their best to comfort her, but Samar was inconsolable. This happened five years and two attacks on Gaza ago. Since 'Cast Lead' in 2008–09, Israel attacked Gaza in November 2012 with Operation Pillar of Defence, and most recently, in July–August 2014 with Operation Protective Edge, by far

They moved from Gaza in the autumn of 2009 so that Samar could receive the rehabilitation therapy she needed. 'If we had stayed in Gaza, Samar would have died,' her father, Khaled, says. 'The facilities have been ruined by the blockade. There is so little to go round.' Samar is sitting with her father, Khaled (37), her mother, Kuther (35), and her siblings Rafet (14), Mohammed (7), Hajar (4) and Sara (2).

the worst attack to date.

How have Samar and her family fared through all their difficulties? I have been wanting to visit her for a long time. Now I have made it, finally.

I am anxious to see what I will find. The man crosses the grass towards the taxi, I open the door, and when it is only half-way open, I hear him calling:

'Dr. Mads, welcome!'

I recognise his face. Khaled walks calmly towards me, we shake each other's hand warmly and look straight into each other's eyes.

'We are waiting! Samar's back from school,' he continues, speaking in his quite respectable French. 'We live there,' he says, pointing at the entrance to the nearest building, number three.

An older man wearing traditional Arab attire opens the door, gives us a friendly nod and lets us in. Khaled points to an open door leading into their flat. Two curious children peer at us from the end of the corridor.

'Our children,' he says, smiling and pointing at them. 'We have more now.'

On my way to the family's new home here in Belgium, I went back over what had happened. Even though I remembered most of the details from my countless lectures about the 2009 Gaza War, I had to check the facts before I left Norway to meet her again in Brussels. The Israeli attack on Samar and her family was thoroughly documented in television news reports by the BBC and Al Jazeera, by Amnesty International and Human Rights Watch, and in the Goldstone Report. Samar's uncle Hassan and her father, Khaled, had retold what happened that day in January 2009.

Around thirty people had sought shelter from the advancing Israeli ground forces on the ground floor of the family's house in the district of Abed Rabbo. Israeli tanks began to shoot at the house, first at the second floor, then at the first floor and finally at the ground floor.

'The house began to shake, and we were all scared out of our wits,' Hassan told the media in 2009. 'The women and the children were screaming with fear because they thought the house was going to collapse on top of them. Since I can speak Hebrew, I shouted out to the Israelis. The officer replied: "Come out!"'

The women and children went out first, with Samar's grandmother waving a white flag.

'The tank was over here,' Khaled told the reporters, as he stood in front of the completely flattened house. 'We were told to come out of the house by an officer with a megaphone: my mother, my wife and my three daughters Samar (4), Amal (2) and Sohad (7). We went outside. An Israeli tank was standing there between seven and ten metres away. We saw that there were two soldiers sitting on the tank; one of them was eating chocolate and the other was eating crisps. We were waiting for orders from the soldiers when a third Israeli soldier came out of the tank carrying an M16 rifle, and he started to shoot at the children. All three were hit by the shots.'

The seven-year-old Sohad was killed on the spot, Amal died later from her wounds, while Samar was shot in the back and was later taken to al-Shifa.

'I carried Amal with her intestines hanging out of her front, then I fetched Samar. The Israeli soldiers killed Sohad with more than ten bullets to the chest. My sixty-year-old mother was hit by two bullets, and she was bleeding. We tried to call for an ambulance, but none came. After a while, we decided to leave the house in small groups. When we left, they shot above our heads. While I was carrying my dead children, the Israeli soldiers came out of their tank and laughed at us. At Zimo Square there was a man with a horse and cart who offered to help us, but they shot both him and his horse. He was evacuated to Egypt, but he died later from his injuries.'

An ambulance only came a few days later to pick up the dead bodies, but the ambulance was destroyed too.

'They were only a few metres away when they shot at us. How could they not see that it was children they were shooting at? They could *see* them,' Samar's uncle Hassan told the BBC journalist Christian Fraser.

Samar only arrived at al-Shifa a few hours later to receive medical attention. The children's mother was not hit. She carried her one dead child. Samar's grandmother, who had been waving the white flag, was hit in one arm and in the stomach.

Uncle Hassan supports Fatah, not Hamas. Both he and Khaled insisted that there were neither Hamas fighters nor weapons in their house.

Samar's two youngest siblings peer up at us inquisitively while we take off our shoes, as is customary. A smell of Arab food greets me: somebody has clearly been waiting for us. Guests are received with the same hospitality in this home as in Gaza, where guests want for nothing, no matter how little money the family may have to spend. There is an expectant mood in the air, as Khaled practically pushes me down the corridor towards the living-room door.

Samar is sitting in a powered wheelchair, occupying the only open space in the crowded living room, with its enormous sideboard, large dining table with six chairs, bookshelves, sofa and bed. The room is full of people. Sitting on the sofa are a European-looking woman in her forties, a man of Moroccan appearance with a dark beard, and a black cat. Khaled and four of his children, aged four to about twelve, stand by the dining table, studying me with their eyes.

Samar looks at me, I meet her gaze and we both smile, perhaps a little bashfully. I recognise her. She has grown: many of her childish features have gone, but she has the same dimple in her right cheek as she did when she was four, and the same gaze, inward-looking, deep and thoughtful. Her raven-black hair is tightly tied in a long, thick plait, with a bright red band of hair elastic at the end, more or less where her blood-stained open wound was five years ago.

I keep a little distance and reach out my hand cautiously. She takes it, giving a slight squeeze, a warm and dry handshake, with no trembling. Her expression is direct and inquisitive. I feel quite overwhelmed, with that helpless feeling you have when you are speechless. I have no idea what to say, so I just stand there, while she – like everybody else in the room – studies me intensely. She wriggles a little in her chair and touches the joystick on the armrest, turning the wheelchair around and moving across towards the corner of the room, as if asking me to follow. I shake hands with everybody in the room. The two adults turn out to be Samar and her family's Belgian lawyer and a Moroccan social worker who has been Samar's support person since she arrived in Belgium in 2009.

I sit down on the edge of a chair next to Samar. We speak softly in French. She is shy and her words vary from childish to very grown-up sentences in a deep, sonorous voice. She tells me that her teacher has just given her a cat as a prize for being the best in her class, and she loves the cat. Its fur is as black as Samar's hair, and it is still young and playful, just like her. She says that she likes it at school and wants to become a vet. She is doing well at school, but they are only allowed to speak French there, not Arabic. Her best friend is from Morocco, and she has many good classmates.

'Mes copines sont très gentilles,' she says in immaculate French. Her friends are very kind.

She playfully corrects grammatical mistakes in my French. Our conversation flows well, and we laugh together. I cannot bring myself to talk about her paralysis, but I ask if she experiences any pain.

'No, I'm fine,' she answers, adjusting her leg by lifting her thigh with both hands. She has braces on both legs, from the thighs down past her knee joints to her ankles, and her feet are tied to the braces with orthopaedic shoes. Her upper body is strong and appears fit, her hands are strong, and her posture is nice and straight.

She is quick to smile, with a kind of confidence, as if she were used to cheering up other people, but her expression keeps descending into one of deep earnestness, as if she were retreating back inside herself.

We are called to the table. I am asked to sit at the head of the table, in the place of honour, with Samar to my left. She elegantly manoeuvres her wheelchair up to the table. Khaled serves the traditional dishes: deliciously spiced roast chicken, rice with nuts, salad, hummus and warm, thin flatbread. He gives me a generous serving,

as is customary. Guests should not want for anything, and food is a symbol of care for others and hospitality. Samar does not eat much but keeps a close eye on what I eat, and how I eat it. There are nine of us at the table, but it works absolutely fine. Some of the children stand, while the adults sit.

The conversation between the adults is mainly concerned with judicial trials and the possibility of taking Israel to court for the killing of the two children and the damage the Israeli shots did to Samar, as well as to their destroyed home. The lawyer says it is a long process, but it is not over yet. She explains that there is a group of lawyers taking things forward.

'I've brought some photos from 2009,' I tell them. 'Would you like to have a look?'

'Yes!' Samar answers immediately.

'Maybe Daddy should take a look first?' I ask carefully.

'Yes, I think I should,' he answers solemnly. Samar shrugs.

We get up from the table. I take out my laptop and find the edited version of the story about Samar. Her younger siblings scramble forth, trying to see, but Khaled pushes them away brusquely. Their father is firm with them when he needs to be. He says that all the pictures are fine, except the one showing the gaping wound in her back.

'She mustn't see that one, but otherwise they're OK,' he says, looking relieved.

'D'accord,' I agree. 'Samar, do you want to sit down with me and have a look?'

She comes to sit close by me, easily turning round her chair in front of the large sideboard, which I can lean back on, while also keeping her curious brothers and sisters at a distance. Samar studies each picture carefully. I do not say much, just telling her what was happening in each specific situation at the hospital. She examines the pictures very intently, leaning forward as far as she can and asking about all the details.

She remembers a lot. She remembers that the boy in the bed next to hers had a large bandage on his stomach and another over his forehead, that the girl in the other bed had a plaster cast and cried a lot. She remembers that she was alone and calling for her mother. She surely remembers many of the ghastly details about the attack itself and the veritable execution of her two sisters, but she does not mention it, and I have no right at all to press her.

'I remember the sweets you brought me,' she says with a beautiful smile. 'That was nice.'

We take our time. Her younger siblings, as well as her elder brother, begin to grow impatient. We have seen enough, so I close the computer screen.

I take out my duty-free bag from Oslo Airport and give Samar some small gifts. We agree that she should share the bag of sweets with her brothers and sisters.

Samar's favourite is the grey rabbit with a pink mouth and its stomach stuffed with sweets.

'It looks like the tiger from last time,' Samar laughs. She strokes its soft fur and looks me straight in the eye. That same expression. The same warmth and intimacy. The same dark abyss.

24. JULY

A CHILDREN'S HOSPITAL IS BOMBED

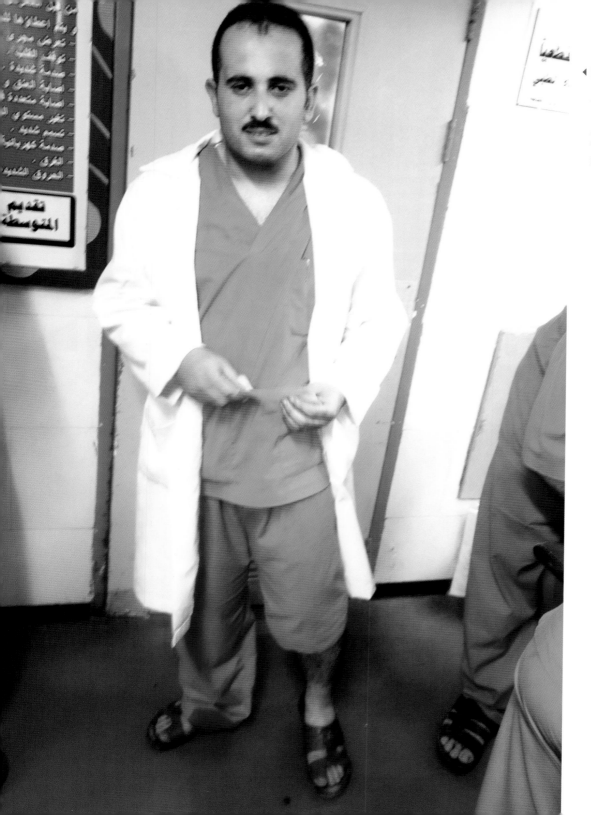

One of the first wounded health workers from al-Durrah Hospital arrives at al-Shifa. The patients and staff all say the same thing: 'The hospital is destroyed. They hit us many times.'

IBRAHIM AL-SHEIKH OMAR, AGED TWO, was a patient at the Mohammed al-Durrah Children's Hospital. This hospital lies to the north-east of al-Shifa, in an area where there had been heavy action. Ibrahim was critically ill and needed ventilator treatment, but the emergency medical team was put out of action by shrapnel and dust from the bombing, and Ibrahim died.

Initially, I could not believe it. The Israelis had certainly bombed other hospitals before, but a children's hospital?

What would have happened if Palestinian forces had attacked an Israeli children's hospital and young patients had lost their lives as a result of the attack? Is there any doubt that the culprits would have been called terrorists?

At a quarter to six, the first ambulance from the children's hospital arrives in the emergency department at al-Shifa. First comes a group of medical workers, some of them in green scrubs, others in white hospital uniforms, a number of them with blood on their clothes, and some with their uniforms torn to shreds. One of them is crying. Some of them are being helped along by colleagues from al-Shifa. They can all walk and talk, so their injuries are not major, but they are all accompanied into the emergency ward to be examined by their careful and painstaking colleagues. Some of them need their wounds seen to, with some needing stitches. Most of them have been hit by pieces of glass or building material when the bombs fell just by the hospital wall, shattering all the windows.

Then come the patients. The first is a young boy, aged maybe two or three, with a cannula in his throat and a terrified expression on his face. He is sitting on the arm of one of the ambulance workers who help with the stream of patients arriving at al-Shifa all day and night. Then more follow in quick succession, patients and staff with different kinds of wounds. Many of the young patients are paralysed with fear.

A grandfather with large bloodstains to the top of his long kaftan gives an angry interview to a local television station. He has not come from the children's hospital himself, but he has evidently heard that it has been bombed.

'The United States are responsible for this. All the bombs falling on us are paid for by the United States. Our children are suffering, our women are suffering, civilians are being bombed and killed,' he says in a strong voice.

The child next to him has a shrapnel wound in his knee and traces of blood on his hospital shirt. The boy is silent, staring out at the world with an empty and bleak expression.

It is now sixteen days since the attacks began. 681 Palestinians have been killed, including 133 children, according to the reports from the Ministry of Health. 4719 have been wounded, including 1375 children. With so many casualties, you would think that the 'contending parties' would take special care with regard to health services, and that the international organisations charged with ensuring that the rules of warfare are followed would be especially vigilant. That is not how things work in Gaza, though. It is starting to dawn on me that healthcare institutions and refugee camps are being directly targeted by the Israeli attacks this time.

The Israeli government forces have already bombed al-Wafa Hospital, Gaza's only hospital specialising in rehabilitation, with chronically ill patients who have major care requirements. In spite of repeated threats from the Israeli commanders and 'warning shots' fired at the hospital with rockets, a group of brave young people from the International Solidarity Movement (ISM) stood their ground at the hospital for several days, acting as human shields. It made no difference. The nurses had to evacuate seventeen disabled, bed-ridden patients in the midst of ongoing Israeli bombing, and the hospital was later completely destroyed.

A few days later, al-Aqsa Hospital was bombed to pieces. Four people were killed and sixty injured. Al-Aqsa Hospital was an important facility for the emergency treatment of casualties in the south of Gaza, where the Israeli attacks have been violent. Naturally, the constant attacks on hospitals are reducing the capacity for treatment in Gaza. Before long, one fifth of hospital beds have been bombed, closed or evacuated as a result of the attacks.

The hospital attacks appear to be systematic and ruthless acts. Even a children's hospital has been attacked now.

That same day, we receive the terrible news from northern Gaza that the UN school in Beit Hanoun has been bombed. It was one of many shelter sites that the UN has established for homeless or evacuated Palestinians. 1200 homeless Palestinians had sought shelter there from – what else but – the Israeli bombardment. The Israeli military leadership had been given the school's precise co-ordinates by the UN through formal channels. The school was mercilessly shelled, and 13 people were killed, including five children, while 150 were wounded, among which were 55 children. Many of them came to al-Shifa over the course of the afternoon on 24 July.

Friday 25 July, 08:10.
I send the following SMS to the Norwegian Minister of Health and Care Services, Bent Høie:

URGENT! Dear Bent Høie, Health and Care Services Minister. The hospitals in Gaza are now being subjected to extensive Israeli military attacks with the loss of human lives, buildings, facilities and capacity. We are asking you, as our superior, and your government, to put into effect immediate measures to establish a physical, uniformed, international presence (UN, ICRC) at the remaining hospitals in Gaza. Patients and staff are now at risk of being killed by Israeli attacks, like the most recent one yesterday evening when the children's hospital in Gaza was bombed. We ask you most urgently to help the Palestinian hospitals, patients and health workers to receive protection in accordance with international law. THE SITUATION IS CRITICAL AND WE ARE ASKING YOU AND YOUR GOVERNMENT TO TAKE THE IMMEDIATE INTERNATIONAL ACTION THAT IS NEEDED. Al-Shifa Hospita, Gaza, 25/07/14. Yours, Mads Gilbert (Senior Clinical Consultant in Emergency Medicine, University Hospital of North Norway) and Mohammad Abou Arab (Senior Consultant, Oslo University

17.57 ▶

A young survivor, a patient from the children's hospital. Terrified, he is being taken care of by one of the many volunteers. The little boy probably has tracheomalacia, a chronic condition that requires a tube to be placed in the throat and into the windpipe to keep it open. After being transferred to al-Shifa, this boy became critically ill with a hospital-acquired infection, his heart stopped and he had to be resuscitated. He is still critically ill and connected to a ventilator at another hospital.

18.16 ▶

One of the many young patients taken into the emergency department at al-Shifa, accompanied by his grandfather. The boy has small shrapnel wounds and is not saying a word.

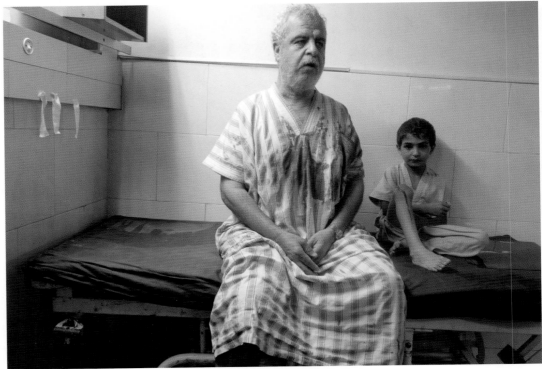

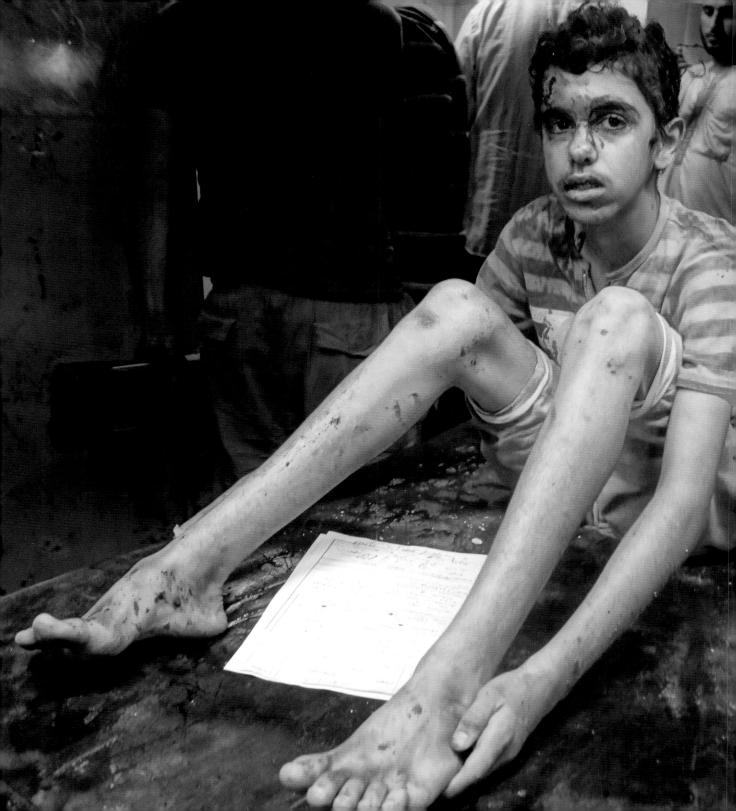

◀ 18.34

I will never forget the expression on the face of this young boy who arrived in the emergency department at the same time as the casualties from al-Durrah Hospital. In all the chaos, I thought he was a patient from the children's hospital, but he had come from another area that had been bombed. It made no difference: all injured children and young people had the same paralysed expression when they arrived at al-Shifa. They had often been separated from their own family in all the panic. All children aged eight or over in Gaza today have experienced four brutal Israeli attacks on their small homeland during their short lives.

▲
25. JULY

We drive through the empty streets on our way to inspect the ruins of al-Durrah Hospital.

FACTS

HEALTH WORKERS KILLED AND WOUNDED

23 Palestinian health workers were killed.

- 16 were on duty
- 7 were at home

83 Palestinian health workers were injured.

- The majority were ambulance workers
- Doctors, nurses, pharmacists and laboratory technicians were also injured

SOURCE: Health Cluster in the occupied Palestinian territory, 'Gaza Strip Joint Health Sector Assessment Report', September 2014.

Hospital). *Cc: Ministerial Secretary General; Director General of Health; Representative Office of Norway to the Palestinian Authority; Managing Director, University Hospital of North Norway.*

Høie's reply comes a little later that afternoon:

Hi Mads! I'm on holiday, but your request for help has been received, and the Directorate of Health is looking into the matter now. The Deputy Minister on duty has been informed. Please do contact her if there is anything else we should know about. Best wishes, Bent

I reply to him immediately:

Thank you very much on behalf of us both for your speedy and positive reply. Mads

And he replies in closing:

No problem! An important issue. Have a good summer!

I am not sure that this summer will be a particularly good one, but our request is then forwarded from the Ministry of Health to the Ministry of Foreign Affairs. Privately, I later learn from sources in the Ministry of Foreign Affairs that it was taken 'to the very top' of the UN system in New York. Unfortunately, it was of little use, if any.

That same day, I go to inspect the damage at al-Durrah Hospital together with Dr. Mohammed al-Kashif, from the Palestinian Ministry of Health, and Dr. Abu Rish, Deputy Managing Director at al-Shifa. We drive off in a rattling ex-ambulance through empty streets, past the smoking ruins of flattened houses. The pungent smell of refuse fills my nose, reminding me of west Beirut in 1982.

We meet the Managing Director of al-Durrah, Dr. Jamil al-Mashri, at the main entrance, together with the porter.

'I'll show you round, but we'll have to be quick. This place isn't safe,' he says, glancing up at the sky.

In every room we pass through – whether it is a doctor's office, an examination room, a treatment room or a normal bedroom – the window panes and metal frames have been blown inside. Shattered glass is strewn everywhere. Most of the ceilings have collapsed, and the walls are knocked down in several places. I see a number of gaping holes in the brick walls, caused by explosions. It is difficult to say whether the hospital was hit directly or by pressure waves and shrapnel from nearby explosions, but I see at least one hole in a wall that must have been caused by a rocket. In any case, the Israelis know what is inside every single building in Gaza, including all the hospitals. This was no accident.

Several of the child-size beds in the intensive care unit have traces of blood on the sheets, where children's dummies and teddy bears have been left in the rush to get out. The resuscitation table where the two-year-old died is also covered with many bloodstains.

I walk through the hospital on my own. A black cat creeps carefully over the sea of broken glass covering the marble floor in the reception. If you want to survive in Gaza, it might be a good idea to be transformed into a black cat, I think to myself; especially if you are a sick or injured child in hospital.

All the offices had been destroyed in a chaotic scene of smashed walls, shards of glass, roofing sheets and window frames. This office had a gaping hole in the wall after the bombing.

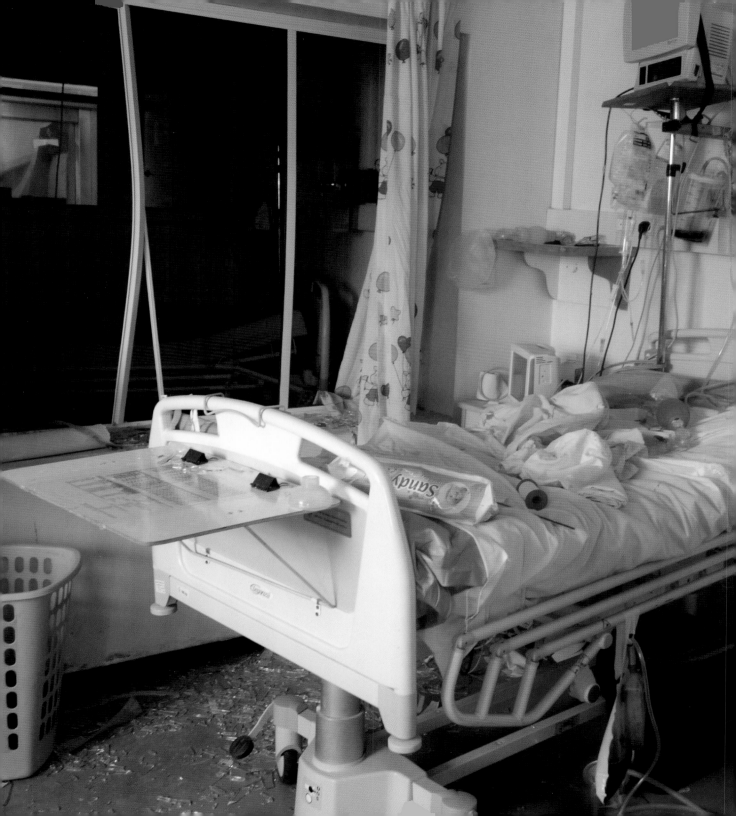

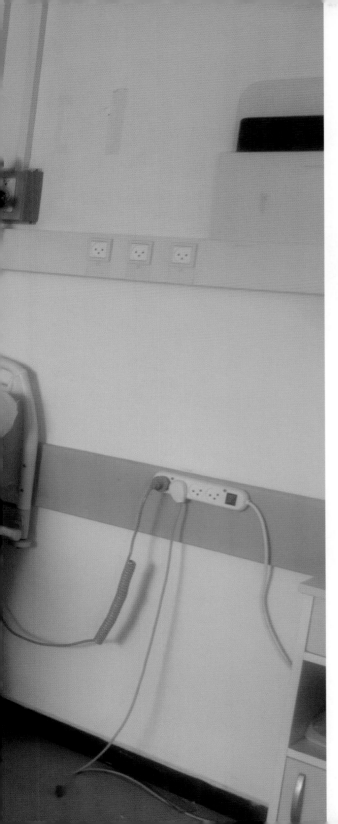

◀ 12.41

The children's intensive care unit at al-Durrah Hospital had been sprayed with broken glass and pieces of shattered furniture. There were stains of blood from the wounded patients in the tiny beds. A critically-ill child who was being resuscitated died during the attack, as the doctors were blinded by the dust and smoke.

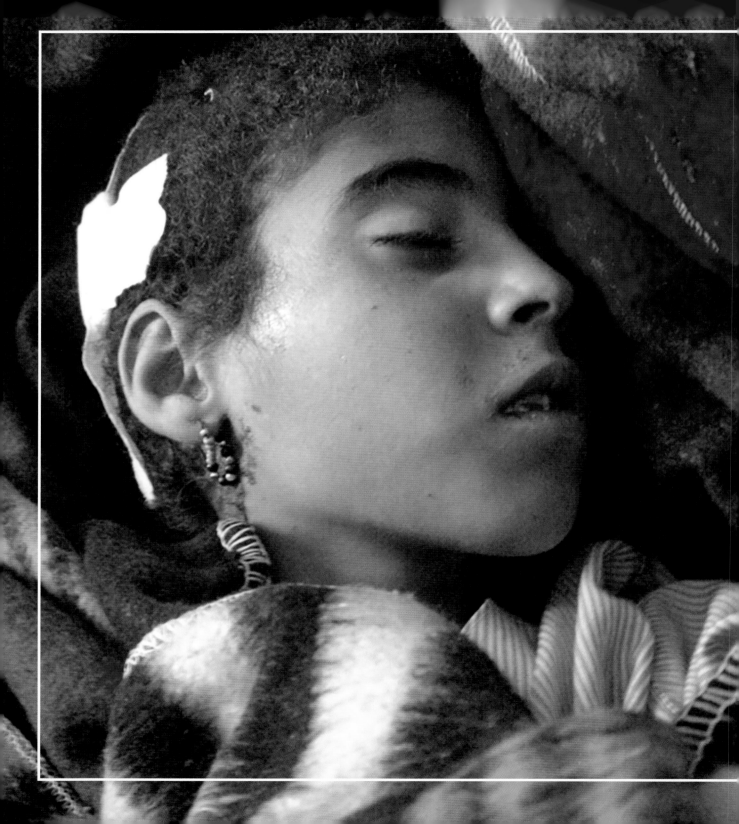

Amal, aged nine, had just arrived at al-Shifa Hospital, exhausted and dehydrated after the Israeli attack at al-Zaytoun. Her father and little brother had been killed in the same attack, and her twin brother Abdallah wounded. Amal had been lying in the ruins for almost three days with other injured relatives, and the dead. The Israeli forces would not let in rescue teams.

PEOPLE OF GAZA
AMAL

THE ISRAELI LEAFLETS FELL ON AL-ZAYTOUN like snowflakes, slightly out of place for July: 'Leave the area, we are going to attack!' Amal knew well from the attacks in 2009 and 2012 that the Israeli threats were real. On both occasions, her neighbourhood of al-Zaytoun, on the southern edge of Gaza City, had been subjected to intense bombardment. Were they about to go through the same thing again? It was now July 2014, and Amal had turned fifteen. She and her twin brother, Abdallah, lived with the rest of their brothers and sisters and their mother in the new home they had built with money raised after the massacre in 2009. That was when her father and little brother had been killed, and her mother had been widowed with many children to look after. Amal was almost killed too, but that was two wars ago now. The attacks were back now, so far in the form of threatening leaflets.

We had met up in June, earlier that summer, just a week before the attacks started. I noticed that both Amal and her twin brother had lost their child-like features, their faces having taken on a more serious and adult look since I had last seen them just after the Israeli attacks in 2012.

'School's going really well,' Amal told me in a quiet whisper of a voice.

We were sitting in the living room at her home together with her mother, drinking sweet tea with *na'nã*, mint.

'Both Abdallah and I are working hard. But my head still hurts. It's not getting better.

Is there something else we can do, Dr. Mads?' Everybody looked at me questioningly.

'We could do another CT scan of your head to see if the shrapnel has moved. Then I could take the images with me to Norway and ask the surgical experts at the hospital in Tromsø. Would you like that, Amal?'

She glanced across at her mother.

'Yes, but only if you come too. And Mum.'

The twins were nine years old when it happened. On 5 January 2009, their father, little brother and at least twenty-five other family members were killed in what is still called the Samouni massacre. The previous evening, the Israeli ground forces had forced around a hundred people from the extended Samouni family inside a warehouse in al-Zaytoun before shutting them in.

At daybreak the next morning, Amal's father wanted to try and persuade the Israeli infantry soldiers to let the family out. The people inside had no food or water and were terrified of what might happen. Her father walked out of the warehouse, holding his youngest son, Amal's little brother, by the hand. He shouted to the Israeli troops, in Hebrew, that all the people inside the building were civilians and had to be let out, and that there were many women and children.

The response from the Israeli soldiers came quickly: Amal's father was shot dead, while her little brother was shot twice in the chest. He bled to death within a few hours.

Not long afterwards, the building was bombed and collapsed. Over twenty family members were killed, many were wounded, while some managed to flee. Amal was left buried in the ruins for the next three days, until her grown-up elder brother, Faraj al-Samouni, found an opportunity to dig her out. For three days, the Israeli forces refused to let the Red Cross or local ambulances rescue the wounded.

A complaint about the massacre was submitted to the Israeli Military Advocate General by an Israeli and Palestinian human rights organisation. The response finally came in May 2012, three years after the massacre. The Israeli military investigated their own actions and cleared themselves of any guilt. Any kind of injustice was denied, and it was flatly dismissed that any reckless or criminal acts had been committed by Israeli forces or officers.

The Israeli forces' actions in warfare, laying siege and carrying out extrajudicial killings are never investigated by independent external institutions or international judicial authorities. Even the worst injustices against the Palestinian civilian population pass without any consequences. Five years on, the Palestinians' demands for an independent judicial inquiry have still not been met.

I first encountered Amal in January 2009, four days after the massacre, during one of my nightly rounds of the paediatric ward at al-Shifa Hospital. She looked like an old woman as she lay there in her hospital

AUGUST 2009 ▶

Amal and two of her cousins outside the tents in al-Zaytoun where the extended Samouni family still had to live half a year after the massacre. The blockade of Gaza means that most buildings destroyed by bombing cannot be reconstructed.

AL-ZAYTOUN, GAZA, JANUARY 2012 ▶

Amal and Abdallah are working hard and doing well at school. Gaza is still trapped behind the Israeli blockade. The painful splinter in Amal's head needs treatment abroad, but she cannot get it.

bed, wrapped up in woollen blankets. Her lips were chapped and dry, and her delicate young body clearly showed signs of extreme dehydration and hunger.

I was at al-Shifa with my good friend and colleague, Erik Fosse, a surgeon from Rikshospitalet in Oslo. Together we had managed to get across the southern border at Rafah to assist the Palestinian health service. Since we were the only foreign doctors there in the first phase of the war, and the Israelis would not let in foreign journalists, the duty also fell upon us to keep the outside world informed of what was happening. The account of the horrific fate of the Samouni family was one of the most brutal we encountered.

I have tried to follow up on Amal and her brother ever since our first meeting in 2009. Every single time I am in Gaza, I go to visit them. This proves impossible when there is a war raging, as moving about outside means risking your life, so I do not leave al-Shifa, apart from taking the few steps needed to walk to the hotel close by. The twins, and their other brothers and sisters, have experienced four brutally violent Israeli wars of aggression over the course of their short lives. They have lost their father and a brother. Both twins have been seriously wounded and have looked death in the face. Since 2009, Amal and her brother have both had pieces of Israeli weapons implanted in their bodies. We removed a painful bullet from one of Abdallah's buttocks in 2012. It is still too dangerous to remove the large piece of shrapnel lodged in Amal's brain.

Still, in spite of all this man-made brutality, both twins have grown into friendly, hard-working and caring people. I feel just as moved every time we meet. The feeling of helplessness against the systematic, cynically planned and repeated destruction of children's lives and living conditions distresses me terribly. The fact that all this is organised by a state which calls itself the 'only democracy in the Middle East', and which accuses others of terrorism, makes it even more upsetting. Most of all, however, I am moved by the children's courage and dignity. It is incredible.

Every single child there has a story, a world of experiences, loss and pain, but also a world of hope, dreams and ambitions for their young lives. Will they have the possibility of realising any of these, or will Gaza be deliberately used as a pressure cooker to foment desperation and senseless violence among young people with no hopes for the future, in order to sustain the old myth of Palestinian 'terrorism'?

Amal and her family were forced to leave their home during the Israeli attacks in the summer of 2014. The leaflets that were dropped were intimidating, and they had bad memories of previous attacks. Their mother managed to rent a house in another part of Gaza until the war was over, and now the family have moved back to their home in al-Zaytoun.

'This is the worst attack we've experienced. They say they want to get Hamas, but then they kill us. We were terrified.'

'It felt better where we'd moved, at least it did until they bombed the mosque,' says Abdallah. 'The shrapnel from the F-16s hit the house we were renting. It was the worst night ever.'

Amal is sitting between her mother and her brother, wearing a black dress and a colourful hijab.

'It was really, really hard for me this time,' she says quietly. 'My head hurt badly during this latest war. The pain wakes me up at night and I can't get back to sleep. I wanted Dr. Mads to come and get us. I told Mum to ring him at al-Shifa and ask him to come, even though I knew he couldn't do anything,' she says.

Her mother says things are better now since the ceasefire in August, but she feels afraid when she sees the news.

'It doesn't give me much faith for a better future,' she sighs. 'Gaza is the best place in the world, but Israel has turned it into a living hell.'

'I wish we had passports,' says Abdallah. 'Then we could all go somewhere safe.'

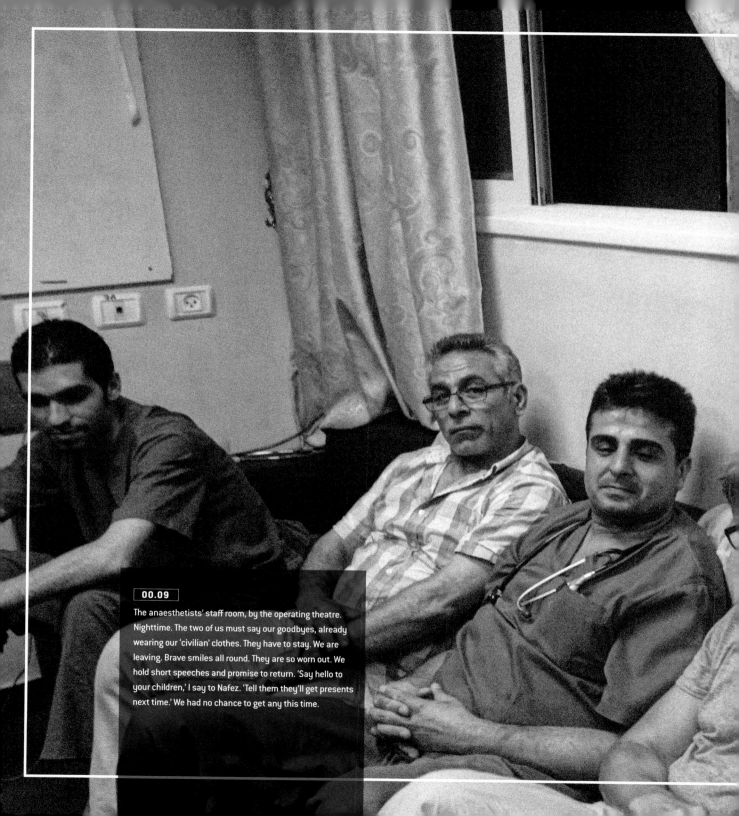

00.09

The anaesthetists' staff room, by the operating theatre. Nighttime. The two of us must say our goodbyes, already wearing our 'civilian' clothes. They have to stay. We are leaving. Brave smiles all round. They are so worn out. We hold short speeches and promise to return. 'Say hello to your children,' I say to Nafez. 'Tell them they'll get presents next time.' We had no chance to get any this time.

MA SALAAM — FAREWELL

IT IS STILL NIGHT IN GAZA.

I have walked the short distance from al-Shifa. The gate is open. Marna House lies in darkness, but it has been brought to life. Refugees from Shuja'iyya have moved in, filling the rooms with families and their lively children. In spite of the terror they have gone through, they are full of energy at all times of day, but nobody has any idea where the families will find new permanent homes for themselves. For now, the hotel and its residents are asleep. I tiptoe up the stairs, for the last time on this occasion.

We are leaving in two hours. For the last time, I have emptied the syringes with their life-saving medications out of the pockets of my green smock. 'K' for ketamine, 'P' for Pavulon, 'T' for atracurium, 'M' for midazolam, 'A' for adrenaline. The extra 10 ml. phial of ketamine for additional doses to soothe the patients' hellish pain. A glass ampoule of adrenaline for forlorn attempts to resuscitate patients bleeding to death. Rolls of gauze used to pack bleeding craters in human bodies ripped to pieces. My final pair of disposable gloves.

Such flimsy tools against such mighty weapons.

They look so fragile as they lie there, a few paltry disposable syringes, so helpless in the fight for life. Symbols of a well-intentioned kind of humanitarianism that eases pain but solves nothing. Has it all been for nothing?

FACTS

FOOD

- Approximately two thirds of the population in Gaza were affected by food shortages and receiving food assistance before the most recent crisis
- 72% were affected by food insecurity or vulnerability to food insecurity
- At least 40,000 people working in the agriculture or fishery sectors were directly affected by the war

Problems with food security and nutrition are due to:

- Loss of income sources (unemployment)
- Loss of agricultural land
- Loss of domestic animals
- Inaccessibility of agricultural land, especially in the 3 km-wide buffer zone along the border
- Inaccessibility of fishing waters on the coastline of Gaza due to the three nautical mile 'fishing border' illegally imposed by the Israeli occupying forces, ruining the Palestinian fishing industry

Most households have a limited ability to purchase food from local markets or to resume food production for subsistence and as a source of income.

SOURCE: OCHA-oPt, 'Gaza: Initial Rapid Assessment', 27 August 2014.

Al-Shifa looks like a lit-up fairy-tale castle. The silence is broken only by the sounds of the drones and a lone cricket. I do not want to leave, and yet I do. The smiling young boy at the little coffee shop kindly asks if I would like some tea. This is the face of Gaza, where children smile even while having to endure so much.

At Marna House, in the room Mohammad and I have been sharing over the past few days. We are incredibly worn out and exhausted. Mohammad is fast asleep. What is he dreaming about? I cannot sleep. Blasts in the distance. Will it never end? How can I leave? I look at myself in the mirror and see how worn out I am. It is time now. Fifteen days will have to do, I think to myself. Erik Fosse is waiting on the Israeli side at Erez, ready to relieve us. Leaving is the right thing to do, but it feels like disloyalty. It is the same every time.

I am a doctor and a clinician. All my working life, I have tried to balance the optimism of active emergency medicine on the one hand – intervening decisively in cases of cardiac arrest or cerebral haemorrhaging, traffic accidents or trauma, self-harm or snowmobile accidents, saving patients' lives and limbs – and, on the other hand, slow but systematic preventative work. This is the social aspect of our work, improving people's living conditions, securing them good homes and clean water, eliminating dangers and reducing traffic speed, making sure children are safe, vaccinated and well nourished. Not least, it means supporting all measures to reduce social inequalities. This is the most important part of our work; it is what makes the medical profession a political tool, providing vital medicine for politics in general.

Of course, when we are threatened by epidemics of lethal illnesses, I have been trained to know that we must immediately identify the harmful agent, in other words the infectious bacterium or virus causing the deadly epidemic. Whether it is tuberculosis, salmonella or Ebola, individual treatment alone will never be enough. Only prevention can save the many: those who have not yet been infected. The lethal contagious matter must be stopped from spreading. This calls for a focus on social conditions: on poverty, living standards, nutrition, hygiene, awareness among the population, importantly, and on the quality of local health services. Advanced air ambulances bringing white people from the rich global north in a valiant struggle to save the infected will not help. It will all be for nothing if significant resources are not also put into more widely reaching preventative work.

Everything I have seen and experienced during the past few weeks in Gaza could have been avoided and prevented. All the death and destruction, all the limbs torn to shreds and people shot to pieces, all the shortages we have been struggling with in the health services, all the bombing of ambulances and hospitals. All this destruction has been one hundred per cent manmade and fully managed by the Israeli government, with the support of US authorities.

Everything we have experienced could have been avoided.

It is no natural disaster or Ebola epidemic that has led to the killing of hundreds of Palestinian children, and the wounding of thousands. It is the result of the Israeli government refusing to choose peaceful, political solutions. They do not want to end their occupation of Palestine or the oppression of the Palestinian people. They would rather expand their own illegal territory with more and more colonies, reinforce their apartheid policies against the Palestinians, continue with their contemptuous blockade and with carrying out regular brutal military attacks on the Palestinians in Gaza and the West Bank.

They know that they have complete military superiority and that the United States will back them, regardless of the atrocities perpetrated. The Palestinians'

FACTS

DESTROYED SCHOOLS

The start of the new school year was postponed from 24 August to 14 September, meaning that 500,000 Palestinian children missed out on important lessons, as well as the security offered by school.

As a result of the Israeli attacks:

- 26 schools were completely destroyed

- 122 schools were damaged, 75 of which are UN schools

- 11 higher education facilities were been affected

SOURCE: OCHA-oPt, 'Gaza: Initial Rapid Assessment', 27 August 2014.

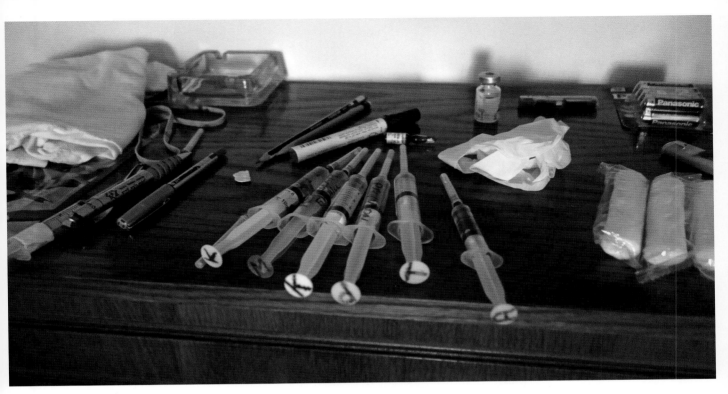

I put my syringes and basic medical kit on the bedside table. Such flimsy tools against such mighty weapons.

backs are up against the wall. They cannot move any further.

All the suffering and destruction I have witnessed in Gaza is what is known in disaster medicine as a purely manmade catastrophe. The occupation, bombardment, siege, destruction, discrimination and oppression are all intentional policies. No doctor or health worker, and no medical system – no matter how good – could dry the torrents of blood running from the Israeli war machine.

Do not send medicine, bandages or field hospitals. Do not say any more words. Do not put victims and oppressors on the same level, or the occupiers and those they occupy.

Stop the bombing, break the siege of Gaza, end the occupation of Palestine.

I have to go home now. I must tell the story and do my part for organised preventative medicine. If Israel wants peace, Palestine must have peace.

If the world is ever to have peace, this hell must not be repeated yet again.

Eventually, I fall asleep.

On our way from Gaza City to the border at Erez in a white, armoured UN vehicle. We are alone on the streets. Everywhere is deserted. The driver has been told to drive fast, while the security officer is in constant touch with his headquarters. 'The situation is volatile,' he says. 'Ceasefires are broken before they start.'

The famous Israeli journalist Gideon Levy comes from Tel Aviv to interview me after I cross the Israeli border. He is a brave man. The café is full of Israeli soldiers in full combat gear, with weapons everywhere. Gideon has a bodyguard and a photographer with him. Dr Erik Fosse met me on the Israeli side of the border at Erez, together with the Norwegian Foreign Ministry officials from the Representative Office of Norway to the Palestinian Authority in Ramallah. Yet another bullet-proof car. Strange that they do not have bullet-proof ambulances in Gaza. They could do with them. It feels that I am now on another planet, where the occupying soldiers can move freely everywhere in full combat gear. Does that make this café a legitimate target? Are the soldiers using the coffee-drinking Israeli civilians as human shields? Several civilian women with small children are sitting at the tables between the soldiers, and the soldiers are carrying their heavy weapons quite openly. Or is it seen as quite natural that those defending a country might move freely around the community and civilian population that they seek to defend?

Still at the same place, we bid farewell to the journalist Gideon Levy and the photographer Alex Levac from *Haaretz*. My smile hides a deep feeling of anxiety. I have just heard about the bombing of the playground at Beach Camp and of al-Shifa. I try desperately to call them. Dr. Sobhi Skaik eventually answers. 'Yes, a rocket has hit the wall around the hospital, but thank God nobody is injured. It's complete chaos here now, though. We've got many casualties from the bombing at Beach Camp.' Dr. Nafez is not answering his mobile, and I am worried his children might have been hit. I should never have left, I think to myself as we drive off along the wide Israeli motorways where all the cars have yellow number plates. The Palestinians' are green, but they are not allowed to drive here. A fully organised apartheid society.

Departure at the airport in Tel Aviv. Erik did not get in, so there would be no changing of the guard. The occupying power is exerting its full control. Victims of the bombing are not to receive any more assistance, and no more medical eyewitnesses will be allowed in.

FOR EVERY NIGHT THERE IS A MORNING

AFTERWORD BY MOHAMMED OMER

IT IS TRUE THAT GAZA HAS been pummelled, maimed, razed to the ground in more areas than not, and its people have endured unbearable times – not only this summer, but in many previous seasons.

But the sunrise comes again and after this winter, spring will be forthcoming. The international community is waking up, reacting and the winds of a more positive time for Palestine are starting to blow. Those innocent children whose blood was spilled in al-Shifa Hospital are the reason for this change. For Sweden and the United Kingdom to begin discussions on the formal recognition of a free and independent Palestine is a courageous step in the right direction. Towards a welcome sunrise that highlights the formidable and obvious difference between the two great forces of power: government on the one side and the unity and determination of grassroots people on the other.

The struggle against an ever-present tyranny and oppression in all aspects of life is not yet over. From the man still opening his falafel shop at 5.00 a.m. for customers, to the students keen to learn who stand at the remains of what was their school gate, and this wonderful lady who rises every morning early to pick what she can from her little lemon tree, to sell and provide some income to feed her children, to the fisherman of forty-six years, who will never leave the sea shore, his trade, his boats and his nets.

Gaza, Palestine, was once known as the Bride of the Mediterranean, and after constant upheavals, bombings and almighty odds, Gaza remains beautiful to this day. This beauty is not just the location, but encompasses the resilience and challenge of its proud and life-loving people and of their next generation who will carry the same dreams and aspirations of a simple, happy life as their parents. These are the open gates through which they will grow and prosper, as before.

Each time the people of Gaza light their candles, to keep away the darkness imposed on them, is a sign of their resilience and of their hope for the next day. Lighting the candle represents their will, as well as being the means to carry on.

Whenever a gate is open for them, Gazans see a glimmer of light shine through. When given one tree to plant they create new growth, as deeply rooted as the ancient olive trees, never letting go of life or the land. A nation which can recycle old spent missiles into flower pots, for buds to bloom in, shows constancy in its dedication to resilience and optimism.

I state this because I know Palestinians. And as determined as we are, I know we are also only human, fallible and flesh and blood, like everyone else. Yet Palestinians, who have been subjected to the longest imaginable occupation, have survived so many wars and daily humiliations and indignities, and still opt – as humans – to remain resilient and act in solidarity wherever they can, despite the odds they face. That's a proud achievement in itself.

Despite factional divisions during this aftermath of another brutal war, the majority of ordinary Palestinian people are united in national history and identity and no one is left to bleed alone. Even when surrounded by devastation, those who are hurt offer support to others. Sometimes, food dishes may be empty but words and gestures of support are plentiful, providing sustenance and unity among the people.

The Palestinians are like two elderly people I know whose home was devastated in the war. The pillars of their house are knocked down, yet they stand together as human pillars, with friends and neighbours rallying to prevent further collapse.

The Palestinian people are mostly youths and children –the people of the sea, the new breeze of our Mediterranean whose stalwart spirit carries hope, determination and, above all, resilience.

In the spirit of young mothers who survived the last war – despite the agony and loss of dreadful conflicts and a still ominous future – hope still bears fruit, and side-by-side they are determined to survive the blight. This too is Palestine in harmony.

A harmony between Gaza's Muslims and Christians during the war, with churches being sanctuaries for all, inclusively. A shared life, through peace and strife, like during so many decades before.

Palestinian history has always been one of sharing, from seeds of grain to loaves of bread shared by neighbours, businesses and imams and priests when their mosques and churches are destroyed and they offer each other sanctuary from the cruel and bitter forces that seek to divide occupied human beings into sub-species. This compassionate sharing is the glue of Palestine and of Gaza.

Heat and pressure, from a nation of occupiers turned bitter, fearful and greedy, only strengthens the glue between occupied Palestinians. The power of memory is strong as it is passed down through the generations, so that as our elders pass through life, the youngsters will also 'remember and never forget' that Palestine is here forever.

'Hope springs eternal...' This too is Palestine.

Mohammed Omer (b. 1984) is a prize-winning young Palestinian journalist living in Rafah, Gaza. He reported daily from Gaza for the international news media throughout the most recent war.

2015: POSTSCRIPT TO THE ENGLISH EDITION

WHEN THE UN SECRETARY-GENERAL Ban Ki-moon visited Gaza on 14 October 2014, not long after the ceasefire, he said that he was there 'with a heavy heart'. He described the destruction of Gaza as 'beyond description', and 'a shame to the international community'.

I share the views of the Secretary-General: the murderous, massive and completely disproportionate attacks carried out by the Israeli government forces against the Palestinian population of Gaza are a historic shame to the 'international community'. For reasons impossible to fathom, the state of Israel seems to enjoy complete immunity in the face of the international legal system and humanitarian law. This apparent impunity is a deep moral, political and ethical problem of our times. The 'West', led by the United States and NATO, uncritically supports the repeated and merciless attacks by Israel that have cost thousands of Palestinian lives and left tens of thousands more wounded for life. A great number of the victims are children.

The UN Secretary-General came to Gaza straight from the international donor conference in Cairo, which had been led by the Norwegian Minister of Foreign Affairs, Børge Brende. The participating countries had pledged 5.4 billion US dollars towards the reconstruction of Gaza. Half a year later, little or nothing has materialised, and no significant reconstruction has begun yet, largely as a result of the continued blockade by Israel – and Egypt. The reconstruction of Gaza's bombed out homes, schools, hospitals, roads, water works, fishing boats, market gardens and factories – to name only some of the structures affected – has barely started. All this is fully in line with Israel's wishes. Israel, the state which had caused the massive destruction of Gaza, did not take part in the donor conference, did not offer any contributions of its own, is never forced to pay war reparations and is never held responsible for its catastrophic military offensives.

The attack on Gaza in July–August 2014 was the fourth since 2006, and the siege of Gaza continues. In a recent report from April 2015, forty-six international aid organisations with extensive experience operating in Gaza concluded that only 26.8% of the funds promised have been released, charges have not been brought against the breaches of international law that occurred, and Gaza is still completely cut off from the West Bank and the rest of the world.

While you read this, the people of Gaza are struggling to find solutions to the enormous humanitarian challenges they face, in a situation constantly aggravated by the Israeli siege. Of course, the blockade should have been lifted long ago. The international solidarity movement is growing in strength and breadth; more and more people are taking part, while our governments continue to offer their tacit support to Israeli state terrorism.

The oppression of Gaza is still a source of shame to the West. Israel's war crimes cannot be allowed to continue.

We are all responsible. We must act while there is still time.

Mads Gilbert
Tromsø, 21 April 2015

ACKNOWLEDGEMENTS

THIS BOOK OWES A LOT TO so many people.

I would like to thank my dear daughters Anna and Siri, as well as their families, for their warm and courageous support during a difficult period, both when I was in Gaza and with all the work and time away that followed. A big thank you is also due to the rest of my family, not least to my sister Sidsel and my nephews Bendik and Eilif, who have followed me closely and with kindness. Thank you for the support and input I have received from close friends and colleagues. Thanks to the dependable members of the Palestine Committee in Tromsø. Kind thanks to Hanne and Morten for their enthusiasm and spirit, and major thanks to Dagfinn for his invaluable assistance with various gadgets and data. Thanks to Linda in Kirkenes, the world's best travel consultant, who always finds a solution. Thank you to Ingrid Evertsen from Senja and Inger Granby from Selbu for the loyal and concrete solidarity work they have been carrying out for the prosthetics workshop in Gaza since 2009.

A big thank you goes to all my workmates at the University Hospital of North Norway (UNN), with special thanks to Nina, Ole Magnus, Knut, Per Øivind and Bård, who always stand up to the challenge when I dash off on assignments in the global south. Thanks to the head of the emergency medicine department at UNN, Jon Mathisen, and to the rest of the management team for their invaluable support. Thank you to my boss, the hospital director Tor Ingebrigtsen, who has supported me thoughtfully and unambiguously, and who manages UNN as a public hospital with global responsibilities, a hospital that has shown long-standing solidarity with the Palestinians.

Special thanks to my close colleague and friend Dr. Mohammad Abou Arab for his courage and strength among the horrors of war, and for his lasting friendship. Thank you to my own private 'agony aunt', Ebba Wergeland, for all her guidance and wisdom over thirty-five years. Thanks to Åse Vikanes and Tor Wennesland for their hospitality and advice, and for the nice times spent with them at the Norwegian Embassy in Cairo. Thank you to Dr. Sobhi Skaik, the medical director of al-Shifa Hospital, and to Dr. Mohammed Kashif, who runs the international section of the Ministry of Health in Gaza.

Many thanks to my two optimistic editors from Kagge Forlag, Tuva Ørbeck Sørheim and Hans Petter Bakketeig, for their sound advice and for the pace at which they worked on developing this project: a pace which was worthy of the emergency medical profession itself. Thank you to the book's Norwegian publisher, Erling Kagge, and thank you to the two creative designers Trine Paulsen and Kim Sølve.

Perhaps my greatest thanks go to my colleagues and all the staff at al-Shifa Hospital and in the ambulance service in Gaza, and to the patients and their families who allowed me to bear witness to their pain, loss, endurance and greatness at such close quarters.

Thank you!

Mads Gilbert
22 October 2014/21 April 2015

METHODOLOGY

THIS BOOK IS NOT WRITTEN AS an academic medical text or as a comprehensive work of documentary writing. Only twelve weeks have passed since I was taking part in the intense clinical work at al-Shifa Hospital in Gaza. Thorough analysis of all the episodes in the war and final, quality-assured figures have not yet been completed. The UN has voted to establish a commission of inquiry this time too; a commission with which the Israeli government refuses to co-operate. It will take time before the documentary evidence has been fully investigated and any potential international trials carried out.

Nevertheless, much is already known, and I have used many sources while working on this book.

Every afternoon, the Palestinian health authorities and hospital management at al-Shifa published confirmed statistics of Palestinian casualties, specifying the numbers of those killed and wounded, which were also sorted by gender and age group, as well as the numbers of health workers killed and wounded, and the number of destroyed health facilities.

Experts from various UN organisations and agencies were continuously situated in Gaza from the beginning of the Israeli attack, known as Operation Protective Edge, in early July 2014 until the ceasefire between Israel and the Palestinian Authority came into effect at the end of August. The UN kept thorough records of Palestinian casualty numbers, as well as the number of internally displaced refugees in Gaza, the extent of destruction to homes, damage to infrastructure, and Israeli military attacks against the UN schools that were the UN's official emergency refugee shelters. The UN also reported on Israeli casualty numbers.

Palestinian and Israeli human rights organisations shed light on individual incidents, violations of human rights and international humanitarian law. The people collecting the data worked in extremely dangerous conditions in order to document the human and social consequences of the Israeli attacks. The use of rockets and other weapons against Israel by Palestinian defence forces was also documented. I referred to these reports daily during my stay in Gaza in order to be able to give as precise information as possible.

8592 people were received by the emergency department at al Shifa Hospital during the 51 days of the Israeli attacks. 490 of these were dying or dead on arrival. 1808 (21.0%) live patients were admitted, of whom nearly 850 required major surgery with anaesthesia in the operating theatres, while 78 died in hospital. Together with colleagues from al-Shifa, we are working on systematic reviews and scientific analysis of the influx of patients, as well as a breakdown of the different kinds of wounds and clinical activity, but this work will take time.

Only some of the documentation I have used is mentioned in the list of sources. My other sources were my own observations and data that I gathered myself at al-Shifa Hospital. I kept records on our clinical work with patients, on the organisation of duties, the difficulties we encountered, and the numerous improvised solutions used by Palestinian health workers in order to cope with the situation. Unfortunately, some of my material was lost in the chaos together with my Moleskine notebook.

With a few exceptions, all the photographs presented here were taken by me or by somebody holding my camera. I carried a small, black Sony Cyber-shot DSC-RX100 compact digital camera with me wherever I went, in a sturdy, black leather case. I am a keen photographer, and I took a mixture of colour and black-and-white stills, only using flash occasionally. The photographs were organised in a database according to the date and time they were taken. All the times given next to illustrations in this book have been taken from the digital timestamps. The images have not been manipulated or processed beyond the rules that apply to documentary photography. Some photographs have been cropped.

As with my previous visits to Gaza, I was able to move freely across the entire hospital, I could speak with whomever I wanted, take photographs of whatever I wished and request any information that might be of interest to me. Nothing I did was monitored by my hosts – the Ministry of Health and the hospital management at al-Shifa – whether during my stay, upon my arrival or departure. As ever, I was thoroughly questioned by the Israeli authorities, although I had nothing physically confiscated by them.

The photographs in this book, as in the book *Eyes in Gaza*, are of key importance as documentary material. It was not always practical to request informed written consent from patients or their families with respect to every single photograph I took, so I have followed the same procedure as in 2009 and for *Eyes in Gaza*. Every single image in this book has been evaluated by senior medical staff at al-Shifa and by the Palestinian Ministry of Health with regard to whether it is ethically justifiable to publish them and to whether patient confidentiality has been respected. I have received official written authorisation for all the pictures included in this book. Names have generally been omitted, both out of consideration for individual patients' safety, and also because circumstances were often extremely complicated and chaotic. There are major cultural differences between an emergency department in a Gazan hospital and one in, for instance, Norway. Palestinian patients and their families are actually keen for their situation to be documented and broadcast, including their physical wounds and the consequences of the military attacks and of the siege. Journalists, with the formal permission required, are able to move about the hospital quite freely, and many patients and their families want to tell their stories. The reason there are few images of women in this book is that it is not considered respectable in Palestinian culture to photograph women, especially with their heads or other parts of their bodies uncovered.

As the proceedings of the commissions of inquiry have not yet been concluded, it is possible that there may be some mistakes, inaccuracies or conflicting figures in the information currently available, and hence also in this book for which I apologise. The overall picture, however, is indisputable.

Abed, Yehia, and Seham Abu Haddaf (2015). 'Gaza War Fatalities and Injuries, 2014: Descriptive Study', abstract of presentation at the Lancet Palestinian Health Alliance (LPHA) Sixth Annual Conference: 'Health of Palestinians', 20–21 March, American University of Beirut.

Abu-El-Noor, Nasser, Ashraf Ajedi, and Mysoon Abu-El-Noor (2015). 'Quality of Life of People Wounded in the Last War (2014) against Gaza Strip', abstract of presentation at the Lancet Palestinian Health Alliance (LPHA) Sixth Annual Conference: 'Health of Palestinians', 20–21 March, American University of Beirut.

AIDA (Association of International Development Agencies) (2015). 'Charting a New Course: Overcoming the Stalemate in Gaza', 13 April. <https://www.oxfam.org/sites/www.oxfam.org/files/file_attachments/bp-charting-new-course-stalemate-gaza-130415-en.pdf>.

Al-Barqouni, Nabil, Mustafa al-Kahlut, Sherin Abed, Loai Albarqouni, and Yehia Abed (2015). 'Impact of the Recent Attack on the Utilization of Medical Services in al-Nasser Pediatric Hospital: A Comparative Study', abstract of presentation at the Lancet Palestinian Health Alliance (LPHA) Sixth Annual Conference: 'Health of Palestinians', 20–21 March, American University of Beirut.

Al-Khayyat, Hana, Lara Abu Sara, Espen Bjertness, and Rita Giacaman (2015). 'Consequences of War on Health: Interviews with Injured Patients from the Gaza Strip Admitted to East Jerusalem Hospitals in the Summer of 2014', abstract of presentation at the Lancet Palestinian Health Alliance (LPHA) Sixth Annual Conference: 'Health of Palestinians', 20–21 March, American University of Beirut.

Amnesty International (2014). 'Families Under the Rubble: Israeli Attacks on Inhabited Homes', 5 November. <https://www.amnesty.org/en/documents/MDE15/032/2014/en/>.

Ashkenas, Jeremy, Archie Tse, and Karen Yourish (2014). 'In Gaza, a Pattern of Conflict', *New York Times*, 31 July. <http://www.nytimes.com/interactive/2014/07/31/world/middleeast/in-gaza-a-pattern-of-conflict.html>.

Bachmann, Jutta, Laurel Baldwin-Ragaven, Hans Petter Hougen, Jennifer Leaning, Karen Kelly, *Önder Özkalipci*, Louis Reynolds, and Alicia Vacas (2015). 'Gaza, 2014: Findings of an Independent Medical Fact-Finding Mission'. <https://gazahealthattack.files.wordpress.com/2015/01/gazareport_eng.pdf>.

Barqouni, N., Y. Abed, H. El Wadia, A. Abu Hamda, H. Madhi, A. Naim, H. El Luch, S. Skaik, Naser Abu Shaban, Nafiz Abu Shaban, S. Signorello, R. Minutolo, and P. Manduca (2015). 'Changes in Newborn Congenital Diseases in Gaza under Attacks: Summary of Findings from Surgery, Maternity and Pediatric Hospitals', abstract of presentation at the Lancet Palestinian Health Alliance (LPHA) Sixth Annual Conference: 'Health of Palestinians', 20–21 March, American University of Beirut.

BBC News (2014). 'Gaza Crisis: Toll of Operations in Gaza', 1 September. <http://www.bbc.co.uk/news/world-middle-east-28439404>.

BBC News (2009). 'Gaza Father Finds Out Child Survived', 21 January. <http://news.bbc.co.uk/1/hi/world/middle_east/7843430.stm>.

Beaumont, Peter, and Hazem Balousha (2014). 'Ban Kimoon: Gaza Is a Source of Shame to the International Community', *Guardian*, 14 October. <http://www.theguardian.com/world/2014/oct/14/ban-ki-moon-visits-gaza-views-destruction-of-un-school>.

B'Tselem (2015). 'Black Flag: The Legal and Moral Implications of the Policy of Attacking Residential Buildings in the Gaza Strip, Summer 2014'. <http://www.btselem.org/download/201501_black_flag_eng.pdf>.

Catron, Joe (2014). 'Gaza Beach Massacre Commemorated by Child Survivors', Electronic Intifada, 10 September. <http://electronicintifada.net/content/gaza-beach-massacre-commemorated-child-survivors/13844>.

Cohn, Marjorie (2014). 'Israel Inflicts Illegal Collective Punishment on Gaza', *World Post*, 15 July. <http://www.huffingtonpost.com/marjorie-cohn/israel-palestine-collective-punishment_b_5589208.html>.

Democracy Now (2014). 'The Untold Story of the Shejaiya
Massacre in Gaza: A Former Israel Soldier Speaks Out', 12
September. <http://www.democracynow.org/2014/9/12/
the_untold_story_of_the_shejaiya>.

Elessi, Khamis, et al. (2015). 'The Impact of the 50-Day
Deliberate Israeli Aggression on Medical Facilities and
Their Staff in Gaza', abstract of presentation at the
Lancet Palestinian Health Alliance (LPHA) Sixth Annual
Conference: 'Health of Palestinians', 20–21 March,
American University of Beirut.

Elessi, Khamis, Yousuf Mokhallalati, Ramy Abdo, and Osaid
Alser (2015). 'The Impact of the 50-Day Israeli Aggression
on Gaza's Children', abstract of presentation at the
Lancet Palestinian Health Alliance (LPHA) Sixth Annual
Conference: 'Health of Palestinians', 20–21 March,
American University of Beirut.

Giacaman, Rita, Rana Khatib, Luay Shabaneh, Asad Ramlawi,
Belgacem Sabri, Guido Sabatinelli, Marwan Khawaja, and
Tony Laurance (2009). 'Health Status and Health Services
in the Occupied Palestinian Territory', The Lancet, 373,
837–849.

Giacaman, Rita, Harry S. Shannon, Hana Saab, Neil Arya, and
Will Boyce (2007). 'Individual and Collective Exposure
to Political Violence: Palestinian Adolescents Coping with
Conflict', European Journal of Public Health, 17, 361–368.

Gilbert, Mads (2014). 'Brief Report to UNRWA: The Gaza
Health Sector as of June 2014'. <http://www.unrwa.org/
sites/default/files/final_report_-_gaza_health_sector_june-
july_2014_-_mads_gilbert_2.pdf>.

Gilbert, Mads (2006). 'Sommerregn i Gaza' [Summer rains
in Gaza], Tidsskrift for Den norske lægeforening, 16,
2136–2139.

Gilbert, Mads, and Erik Fosse (2013). Eyes in Gaza, updated
edition. Translated by Guy Puzey and Frank Stewart.
Quartet, London, (first English-language edition published
2010). Originally published (2009) as Øyne i Gaza.
Gyldendal, Oslo, 2009.

Gilbert, Mads, and Erik Fosse (2009). 'Inside Gaza's al-Shifa
Hospital', The Lancet, 373, 200–202.

Gilbert, Mads, and Sobhi Skaik (2015). 'Some Medical
Consequences of the Israeli Operation "Protective Edge"
2014: Preliminary Data from al-Shifa Hospital, Gaza
Occupied Palestine', abstract of presentation at the
Lancet Palestinian Health Alliance (LPHA) Sixth Annual
Conference: 'Health of Palestinians', 20–21 March,
American University of Beirut.

Gilbert, Mads, and Sobhi Skaik (2013). 'Patient Flow and
Medical Consequences of the Israeli Operation Pillar of
Defence: A Retrospective Study', The Lancet, 382, S13.

Haaretz (2014). 'UN Rights Chief: Israel Defying International
Law in Gaza, Must Be Held Accountable', 31 July. <http://
www.haaretz.com/news/diplomacy-defense/1.608237>.

Health Cluster in the occupied Palestinian territory (2014).
'Gaza Strip Joint Health Sector Assessment Report',
September. <http://reliefweb.int/sites/reliefweb.int/files/
resources/Joint_Health_Sector_Assessment_Report_Gaza_
Sept_2014.pdf>.

Heszlein-Lossius, Hanne, Yahya al-Borno, Yasmeen Keita,
Nashwa Skaik, Hazim Shawwa, and Mads Gilbert (2015).
'Israeli Drone Attacks on Gaza Cause Severe Amputation
Injuries: A Retrospective, Clinical Follow-Up Study of
Traumatic Amputees in Gaza, Occupied Palestine', abstract
of presentation at the Lancet Palestinian Health Alliance
(LPHA) Sixth Annual Conference: 'Health of Palestinians',
20–21 March, American University of Beirut.

Human Rights Watch (2014). 'Israel: In-Depth Look at
Gaza School Attacks', 11 September. <http://
www.hrw.org/news/2014/09/11/israel-depth-look-gaza-
school-attacks>.

Manduca, Paola, Iain Chalmers, Derek Summerfield, Mads
Gilbert, and Swee Ang (2014). 'An Open Letter for the
People in Gaza', The Lancet, 384, 397–398.

Maqadma, M., H. Wesley, G. al-Jadba, I. El-Bursh, M. Shaker,

W. Zeidan, and A. Seita (2015). 'Health of Internally Displaces Persons in Temporary UNRWA Shelters during the 50 Days of War in Gaza', abstract of presentation at the Lancet Palestinian Health Alliance (LPHA) Sixth Annual Conference: 'Health of Palestinians', 20–21 March, American University of Beirut.

Masi, Alessandria (2014). 'Massacre in Gaza's Shejaiya Market: At Least 27 Palestinians Killed as Cease-Fire Ends', *International Business Times*, 30 July. <http://www.ibtimes.com/massacre-gazas-shejaiya-market-least-27-palestinians-killed-cease-fire-ends-1643568>.

Mondoweiss (2014). 'Statement: Legal Experts and Human Rights Defenders Demand International Community End Israel's Collective Punishment of Gaza', 28 July. <http://mondoweiss.net/2014/07/international-collective-punishment>.

OCHA-oPt (United Nations Office for the Coordination of Humanitarian Affairs, occupied Palestinian territory) (2015). 'Fragmented Lives: Humanitarian Overview 2014'. <http://www.ochaopt.org/documents/annual_humanitarian_overview_2014_english_final.pdf>.

OCHA-oPt (2014a). 'Gaza Strip: Damaged Clinics as of 5 Sept. 2014'. <http://www.ochaopt.org/documents/GazaStrip_ClinicsHospitals_A4_V1.pdf>.

OCHA-oPt (2014b). 'Gaza: Initial Rapid Assessment', 27 August. <http://www.ochaopt.org/documents/gaza_mira_report_9september.pdf>.

OHCHR (United Nations Office of the High Commissioner for Human Rights) (2014). 'UN Commission of Inquiry on Gaza Hears Moving Testimony, Seeks Access', 23 December. <http://www.ohchr.org/EN/NewsEvents/Pages/DisplayNews.aspx?NewsID=15456&LangID=E>.

Palestinian Centre for Human Rights (2014a). 'Urgent Appeal to Palestinian President and Government: PCHR Warns of Consequences of Fuel Shortage at Gaza Hospitals and Expected Suspension of Health Services at UAE Red Crescent Hospital', 21 October. <http://www.pchrgaza.org/portal/en/index.php?option=com_content&view=article&id=10681>.

Palestinian Centre for Human Rights (2014b). 'Initial Statistics of Attacks on Basic Service Facilities & Forcible Displacement in the Gaza Strip', 2 August. <http://www.pchrgaza.org/portal/en/index.php?option=com_content&view=article&id=10556>.

Perry, Mark (2014). 'Why Israel's Bombardment of Gaza Neighborhood Left US Officers "Stunned"', Al Jazeera America, 27 August. <http://america.aljazeera.com/articles/2014/8/26/israel-bombing-stunsusofficers.html>.

Punamäki, Raija-Leen, Samir Qouta, and Eyad El-Sarraj (2001). 'Resiliency Factors Predicting Psychological Adjustment after Political Violence among Palestinian Children', *International Journal of Behavioral Development*, 25, 256–267.

Shelter Cluster Palestine (2015). 'Shelter Cluster Factsheet', March 2015. <http://www.shelterpalestine.org/Upload/Doc/d79e33fc-fd4d-4bc8-859d-920580a7ee3b.pdf>.

Shuttleworth, Kate, and Hazem Balousha (2014). 'Qatar Is Top Donor as $5bn Is Pledged to Rebuild Gaza', *Guardian*, 12 October. <http://www.theguardian.com/world/2014/oct/12/gaza-rebuild-international-donors-israel-hamas-qatar>.

Solberg, Kristin (2014). 'Gaza's Health and Humanitarian Crisis', *The Lancet*, 384, 389–390.

UNRWA (United Nations Relief and Works Agency for Palestine Refugees in the Near East) (2015). 'Gaza Situation Report 78', 5 February. <http://www.unrwa.org/newsroom/emergency-reports/gaza-situation-report-78>.

WHO (World Health Organisation) (2014). 'Situation Report: Gaza Crisis', Issue 1, 10 July. <http://www.emro.who.int/images/stories/media/Sit_report_oPt.10_July_2014.pdf.pdf?ua=1>.

Yaghi, Mohammad, Arild Vaktskjold, Osama A. Balawi, Mahmoud Deeb Daher, and Wendy Venter (2015). 'The Mortality in the Gaza Strip in the Period July–September 2014', abstract

of presentation at the Lancet Palestinian Health Alliance
(LPHA) Sixth Annual Conference: 'Health of Palestinians',
20–21 March, American University of Beirut.

Yourish, Karen, and Josh Keller (2014). 'The Toll in Gaza
and Israel, Day by Day', *New York Times*, 15 July
(updated 8 August 2014). <http://www.nytimes.com/
interactive/2014/07/15/world/middleeast/toll-israel-gaza-
conflict.html>.

ADDITIONAL SOURCES

Daily updates and casualty statistics from the Ministry of
Health, Palestinian Authority, Gaza. (See e.g.: <http://www.
moh.ps/attach/684.pdf>).

Israeli Defence Forces. <http://www.idf.il/english/>.

Israeli Ministry of Foreign Affairs. <http://www.mfa.gov.il/MFA/>.

Palestinian Central Bureau of Statistics. <http://www.pcbs.
gov.ps/>

UNDP (United Nations Development Programme).

UNICEF (United Nations Children's Fund).

UNRWA (United Nations Relief and Works Agency for Palestine
Refugees in the Near East).

Weekly reports, humanitarian updates and humanitarian
snapshots (July–August 2014) published by OCHA-oPt
(United Nations Office for the Coordination of Humanitarian
Affairs, occupied Palestinian territory). <http://www.
ochaopt.org/>.

WHO (World Health Organisation).

The quotation by Desmond Tutu, 'If you are neutral in situations
of injustice, you have chosen the side of the oppressor', appears
in *Ending Poverty as We Know It: Guaranteeing a Right to a Job
at a Living Wage* by William P. Quigley (Temple University Press,
Philadelphia, 2003), p. 8.

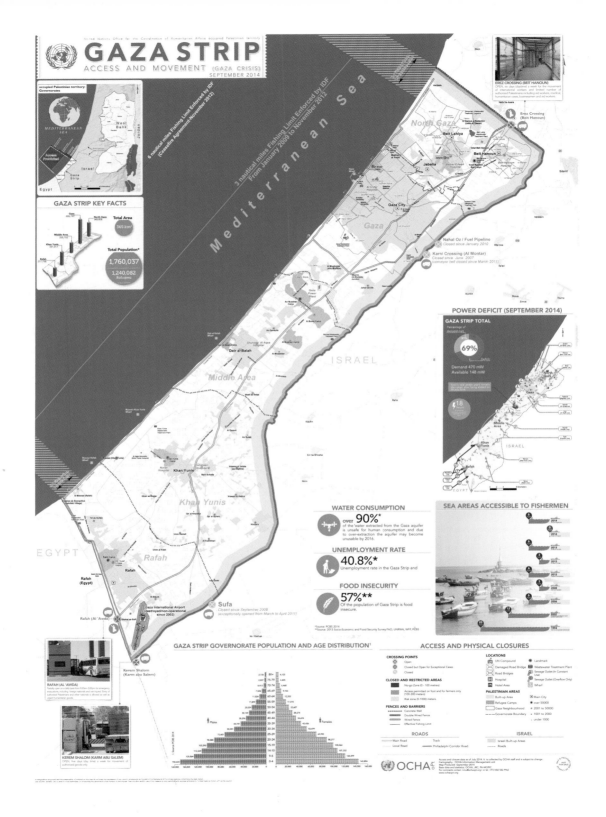